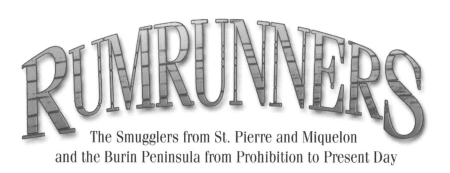

RUMRUNNERS

The Smugglers from St. Pierre and Miquelon
and the Burin Peninsula from Prohibition to Present Day

J. P. ANDRIEUX

FLANKER PRESS LTD.
ST. JOHN'S
2009

Library and Archives Canada Cataloguing in Publication

Andrieux, Jean-Pierre
   The rumrunners : from the days of prohibition to
rumrunning on the Burin Peninsula / J.P. Andrieux.

Includes bibliographical references and index.
ISBN 978-1-897317-48-8

   1. Smuggling--Saint Pierre and Miquelon--History--20th century.
2. Smuggling--Newfoundland and Labrador--Burin Peninsula--History--
20th century. 3. Prohibition--United States--History--20th century.
4. Saint Pierre and Miquelon--History--20th century. 5. Burin Peninsula
(N.L.)--History--20th century. I. Title.

HV5091.S24A534 2009   364.1'33   C2009-904639-3

PRINTED IN CANADA

Cover Design: Adam Freake

FLANKER PRESS
PO BOX 2522, STATION C
ST. JOHN'S, NL, CANADA
TOLL-FREE: 1-866-739-4420
WWW.FLANKERPRESS.COM

14 13 12 11 10 09   1 2 3 4 5 6 7 8 9

Canada Council   Conseil des Arts
for the Arts   du Canada

We acknowledge the financial support of: the Government of Canada through the Book Publishing
Industry Development Program (BPIDP); the Canada Council for the Arts which last year invested $20.1
million in writing and publishing throughout Canada; the Government of Newfoundland and Labrador,
Department of Tourism, Culture and Recreation.

Dedicated to
Bill McCoy, also known as the Real McCoy,
premier rumrunner of the American Prohibition era

Also by J. P. Andrieux

Marine Disasters and Shipwrecks: Volume I

CONTENTS

INTRODUCTION

The Bahamas, Bermuda, Belize (formerly British Honduras), and St. Pierre and Miquelon had a great deal in common during the era of Prohibition, when they were offshore bases in strategic positions as distribution centres for the liquor trade to the United States.

As well as acting as a huge warehouse for alcohol from Europe, St. Pierre's convenient location just off Canada and its close proximity to the U.S. made it a haven for Canadian distributors to set up operations to service their American clients.

The Americans were chiefly interested in rye and bourbon whiskies, and Canadian distillers were anxious to fill a void caused by the Eighteenth Amendment of the U.S. Constitution. This prohibited the distillation and consumption of alcohol in the U.S. Distillers could now supply from their offshore bases.

As a result, St. Pierre became one of the chief liquor supply sources for dry America during the period.

After a postwar period of cross-border smuggling, the Canadian Government, bowing to pressures from the United States Government, amended the Canada Export Act, which among other things forced Canadian distillers to export their liquor to a country that wasn't under prohibition and to put up a bond that could only be refunded once a bona fide landing certificate, proving the goods had been landed, was stamped by customs officials. As a result, the traffic in St. Pierre boomed.

During that period, local laws also made Canada dry. St. Pierre was also the supply base for alcohol that would end up in Quebec, New Brunswick, Prince Edward Island, Nova Scotia, and Newfoundland.

The traffic to the U.S. stopped with the Twenty-First Amendment, known as repeal, in 1933. It lasted to a much lesser degree in the Canadian/Newfoundland areas until the beginning of hostilities of World War II stopped it. The Newfoundland traffic in effect always continued, even after Confederation in 1949, in small proportions due to the proximity of St. Pierre to the Newfoundland coast, a mere twelve miles away.

In 1988, the lone Royal Canadian Mounted Police patrol vessel based on the Burin Peninsula was removed. In effect, it gave the rumrunners from the area *carte blanche* to smuggle liquor and tobacco into Newfoundland. The trade was now wide open and the volume of goods that entered Newfoundland resembled a smaller version of Prohibition.

This book, with an abundance of photographs, is divided into two sections, one covering the American Prohibition era and afterward, and the Newfoundland trade that has always existed, up to the Terrenceville raids when "proceeds of crime" legislation was used to bring to an end, or near-end, to the rumrunning tradition and tobacco smuggling between St. Pierre and Miquelon and Newfoundland.

The island of St. Pierre as seen from the tip of the Burin Peninsula.
(Author collection)

Green Island and the Burin Peninsula in background as seen from St. Pierre.
(Author collection)

PROHIBITION SETS THE STAGE

Alcoholic beverages have always played a well-defined role in the social life of Canada and the United States. "Strong drink" has been the target of countless denunciations, the subject of sermons without number, and the whipping boy of tract publishers and book writers. Nonetheless, distilled beverages have all the while been commonplace, and even indispensable ingredients of such diverse human undertakings in North America as barn-raising bees, harvesting, socializing and to celebrate the successful conclusion of business deals. As well, whisky and brandy, in particular, have long had medicinal properties attributed to them, and they are still prescribed as such today.

The distillation of whisky started in Pennsylvania in 1760. Thirty-four years later, when the federal government placed a tax of $0.09 a gallon on all distilled spirits, it resulted in the Whisky Insurrection of 1794.

As always, there were those who opposed the use of intoxicating liquor. By 1800, they were becoming a factor of some importance.

PROHIBITION

The first formal Temperance Society in the world was organized in Moreau, New York, in 1808. It was called the Union Temperance Society of Moreau. It lasted a few years, and though it was relatively unsuccessful, it encouraged other reform movements. Several other societies sprang up in various states. During the next decade, mostly to promote moderation rather than total abstinence, they had a short life and did little to improve conditions.

Drinking created many nuisances. Early laws were not against the use of intoxicants but against their misuse.

Efforts of New England preachers including Reverend Lyman Beecher, father of Harriet Beecher Stowe, succeeded in revitalizing the Temperance Movement in 1826. Beecher's sermons on the subject carried wide circulation and their influence was great. As a result, Temperance Societies mushroomed and resulted in formation of the American Temperance Union, grouping some 8,000 societies, most of which had some affiliation with the national organization. Several members of Congress joined it, giving it far greater prestige. Temperance finally became a religious issue. The movement grew and with it the advocation of total abstinence.

Various cities, of which Portland, Maine, was the first major one, managed to pass local option laws preventing the sale of liquor. In 1847, the U.S. Supreme Court ruled that the state had full power to regulate or prohibit the sale of intoxicating liquor. This gave great impetus to movements for statewide prohibition.

As a means of establishing additional revenue during the U.S. Civil War, the Internal Revenue Act established a tax on each liquor dealer and manufacturer, and this became an important source of revenue. As a result, temperance leaders had to combat the argument that prohibition would cause the government a great loss of income.

Until the mid-1800s, the temperance movement had been effected entirely by men. In 1852, women became interested. By 1870, the women's crusade was inspired and began marching on saloons, causing considerable commotion. As a result of the women's crusade, many thousands of saloons closed, as well as breweries. The collection of liquor taxes by the federal government dropped substantially. The crusades did not affect the laws that permitted saloons to operate, or the alliance between liquor interests and politicians. While things soon returned to normal, the campaign served to revive national interest in the issue of temperance. The most important outcome was organization of the National Women's Temperance Union in 1874, the goal of which was the legal prohibition of all intoxicating liquor. Under the later guidance of Frances Willard, it became the most powerful temperance organization in the world.

The first constitutional amendment for prohibition to be submitted to Congress was introduced in the House in 1876, but was buried in committee. Successive efforts met a similar fate, and it wasn't until 1914 that another amendment went before Congress.

The anti-liquor forces met plenty of resistance from the distillery and brewing interests. The latter used it for propaganda, but like their adversaries were in a tug-of-war between the two opposing factions.

In 1895, the Anti-Saloon League of America was formed. It took a further ten years to become effectively organized over a nationwide area. It had paid, full-time employees and adequate documentation of the entire anti-liquor crusade. Throughout the country this league became powerful and eventually achieved national prohibition.

To be effective, the League realized it needed greater congressional support and concentrated its efforts in Congress. By the time of the 1916 election, the fight for prohibition had been all but won.

On September 8, a law was passed which forbade the manufacture of distilled liquors. Finally, the advocates of the Eighteenth Amendment succeeded in bringing the matter to vote. It was approved sixty-five to twenty. Several amendments were brought forward to ensure that Congress and several states would have concurrent power to enforce this article. In its final form the House voted 282 to 128, on December 18, 1917.

The Eighteenth Amendment, having been adopted by Congress, went to the states for ratification. Mississippi was the first to ratify, on January 8, 1918. Nebraska, the thirty-sixth state, did so on January 14, 1919. The war was without a doubt a factor in the speed in which this ratification was accomplished. Prohibition became the law of the land effective one year later.

In October of 1919, the National Prohibition Act, usually called the Volstead Act, was passed by Congress, vetoed by President Wilson, but it passed over his veto. The act was designed to provide the enforcement apparatus for the Eighteenth Amendment and placed the administration of the law under the Bureau of Internal Revenue, a subdivision of the Treasury Department. John F. Kranes of Ohio was appointed the first Commissioner of Prohibition.

The advent of Prohibition was hailed by the majority as the solution to most of the problems of mankind. Little did the American people envision the problems which Prohibition would engender. This period of National Prohibition, which the nation suffered, challenged each individual American. It also became a challenge to Congress, state

Congressman Andrew Volstead, the Father of Prohibition. (Photo courtesy of the U.S. National Archives 306 – NT – 87793)

governments and courts, local and state police, the clergy, customs, and prohibition activists. The experience known as the Great Noble Experiment proved to be one replete with lessons for posterity. Never before had the power of the underworld directly or indirectly touched such a tremendous portion of the U.S. citizenry.

Agents were ready for enforcement. On the morning of the first day of Prohibition, agents seized quantities of liquor. From this point forward the Prohibition Law was broken on a widespread scale during every minute of that period, despite everything the federal government and its agencies could do in an effort to prevent it.

Once liquor was legally banned, it seemed to gain in desirability. Speakeasies sprang up like mushrooms. Business became very lucrative. Citizens who were otherwise law-abiding patronized the speakeasies, and they became lawbreakers.

Liquor was made available in the U.S. from three different sources – bathtub gin, liquor that had been hoarded in warehouses, and the liquor that entered the country from outside its borders. The best quality of liquor came from the third source.

The Department of Justice had made no particular preparations to handle violators of the Volstead Act. Only a few cases were expected, but in only a few months the federal courts in the country were overwhelmed by the number of cases awaiting trial. Penitentiaries could hardly hold the rumrunners, bootleggers, and others who had been arrested.

Corruption among some of the prohibition agents is a matter of public record. Certainly the generous offers from rumrunners and bootleggers were highly tempting to law enforcement personnel. Many succumbed to the temptations. It is said that the so-called government bootleggers were free from molestation.

Prohibition brought about a great change in New York, and particularly along Broadway. Many famous hotels and cabarets found it necessary to go out of business, for in the past, differences between profit and loss had largely depended upon the liquor sales. New ones were set up, but gradually came under domination of criminal elements that acquired control over the flow of liquor in the city.

The upsurge of the underworld as a result of Prohibition was undoubtedly its most vicious development. This was the element which in large part eventually controlled the great flow of liquor from the sea, which was to become one of the greatest problems of the period, and the particular concern of the U.S. Coast Guard.

Hijacking and double-crossings were common, the stories of the rise of gangsters such as Al Capone and John "Legs" Diamond were the most famous, and the fortunes they amassed and the activities in which they engaged constituted harmful by-products of Prohibition.

There were about 70,000,000 gallons of liquor in warehouses at the outset of Prohibition. Under special dispensation, certain distilleries were permitted to continue production for uses other than beverage. Medicinal liquor was removed from warehouses in large quantities. Alcohol was manufactured by licensed distilleries placed in bonded warehouses and sold by the government.

Industry under these classifications, in large and increasing quantities and production, was underestimated. Much of the pure alcohol which was manufactured found its way into the illicit liquor trade. Many new companies came into existence which never manufactured anything before. However, this later fell off.

Persons smuggling spirits by sea had certain advantages, since liquor was not contraband until it had actually crossed the border into the United States. The flood would soon start from the sea, and the Coast Guard didn't have the personnel to stop it effectively. A flood of liquor would eventually follow in from off shore.

Customs clearance granted for the high seas to a rumrunning schooner listing her cargo. The *Almeida* was owned by Henri Moraze.
(Document courtesy of Mr. Henri Moraze.)

EARLY SMUGGLING TO CANADA AND NEWFOUNDLAND

North of the border, in Canada, proscription against *eau de vie* went back to the earliest days of French Canada. Bishop Laval and the Jesuit missionaries crusaded to keep whisky away from the Indian fur trade in the nineteenth century, as an appeal to conscience. It was not a widespread success in curbing the use of whisky, and the call finally came for a legal proscription. In 1878, the Canada Temperance Act, commonly known as the Scott Act, became a local-option law and the matter was taken to the municipal ballot boxes. Pressure was applied to politicians by organizations such as the anti-drunk crusaders, in their battle to outlaw alcoholic beverages.

Meanwhile, in the second part of the 1800s, there was a thriving smuggling trade established between St. Pierre and Miquelon, the French-owned islands off the southwest coast of Newfoundland and what was then Upper Canada. It has been ascertained that half the spirits and tobacco consumed in Lower Canada were smuggled from the French colony.

The following account of the clandestine trade taken from a Montreal newspaper of the day shows the methods used:

> "Some Newfoundlanders are in the trade; they sail from St. Pierre to some unfrequented part of Canadian Labrador, where in foggy weather they meet smaller crafts. These smaller boats again tran-

ship their cargoes into punts and dories farther up the St. Lawrence, and lastly it is distributed by farmers in carts. It is an immense business and has enormous evil effects on French Canadians."

Icebergs made it very difficult for early rumrunners to ply their trade.
(Author collection)

With the disappearance of icebergs and the opening of the navigation season in the St. Lawrence (River) between Quebec and the Gulf, so-called bold smugglers of the north would again be brought to public attention by the persistence in which they resumed their traffic of former seasons, and the readiness with which they fought when attacked or punished by vessels of the Canadian customs fleet.

The headquarters of the smugglers of the St. Lawrence and New England ports was on the French Islands of St. Pierre. Hitherto, their chief traffic had been liquor. However, toward the end of the 1800s, they extended their operations and ended up doing a large business in tobacco, the French Government having reduced the duties on all classes of tobacco landed in St. Pierre. The new duty, amounting to $0.41 for 100 pounds, meant that St. Pierre was practically a free port for the entry of tobacco, so that smuggling it from there to Boston, Quebec, or more convenient ports on the Atlantic Coast or shores of the St. Lawrence was now quite profitable for coasters.

Liquor was admitted into St. Pierre free of duty. A trio of large three-masted schooners was constantly employed by the smugglers to carry cargoes of alcohol sixty overproof from Boston to St. Pierre. There was no concealment about this part of the traffic. The difficulty consisted in landing the alcohol in Canadian ports so as to avoid the duty of $2.00 a gallon. There were two and sometimes three transhipments of the liquor from the time it left St. Pierre until it was safely put ashore upon the banks of the St. Lawrence. The rumrunners' profit from the traffic is illustrated by the fact that the whisky or alcohol, which was the chief staple of the trade, sold for over $1.40 in Boston, but with the duty added sold in Canada for no less than $3.75 a gallon. Jamaican rum and French liquors and brandies were also admitted duty-free into St. Pierre and formed a portion of most cargoes of the smuggling schooners from St. Pierre to Quebec and other points. As the Canadian duties upon these was very high, there was even more profit in smuggling these commodities compared to that of whisky or alcohol.

The large gulf schooners that left St. Pierre with liquor aboard never risked a total loss of vessel and cargo by venturing as far as Canadian inland waters. Before leaving the Gulf for the mouth of the St. Lawrence River, they were each met by three or four smaller crafts, generally schooners of very small value, which divided among them the cargo of the large craft. One of these may be seized or confiscated, yet the profit from the operations of the others made

A cache of cases of alcohol discovered in the woods off the St. Lawrence River.
(Photo courtesy of the RCMP Archives)

the entire trip a lucrative one, and often they all escaped capture. Smaller boats landed the liquor from the schooner, often under cover of night, at some of the parishes of the island of Orleans in Quebec, or elsewhere in the vicinity.

Some parishes of the Lower St. Lawrence had become completely demoralized by the proportions by which this traffic had grown. Farmers completely neglected their land and fishermen their nets, to engage in smuggling ventures that promised large returns. The parish priests complained bitterly of the demoralizing effects upon their people and of the fearful drunkenness that prevailed whenever Whisky Blanc, as the fiery alcohol was called by French Canadians, was landed and sold. In fact, many of the country priests would become informers and report smugglers to the government.

There is no doubt that encouragement was given to the smugglers by the failure of the justice system to subdue the noted smuggler Captain Bouchard, who fought and compelled the retreat of a government revenue cutter. He was only subdued and captured after he had been besieged in and dislodged from the smugglers' stronghold on Isle aux Coudres in the Lower St. Lawrence. Yet, when his case was brought to trial in the early 1890s, he was only convicted before the court of simple assault and got off with a fine of $25.00.

In another case, the government cruiser *Constance* was defied by the crew of a little smuggling schooner on the St. Lawrence River. The schooner in question was the *Steadfast,* registered in St. John's, Newfoundland. She refused to come to when summoned in the Queen's name, and when about to be boarded by government officers, her crew fought with their axes and wounded a couple of them. Finally, the prize, with her cargo of $15,000 worth of liquor, was secured and her crew put in irons. Two other schooner companions were able to escape arrest safely and probably landed their cargoes.

By the turn of the century, successive decisions by the Privy Council in London had established that control over liquor sales in Canada at retail levels was a provincial matter. Manufacture, import, and export remained in federal hands. However, neither level of government was particularly anxious to enforce the Canada Temperance Act, which decreed that responsibility for Prohibition lay with the municipality and depended upon a local vote. The law was only marginally successful, as one locality might vote dry while its neighbour opted for the sale of liquor. Since political popularity could be jeopardized by a wrong stand, politicians condemned alcohol on the one hand, but turned a blind eye to plugging loopholes that would anger the wets.

When the First World War ended in November of 1918, there was fear that returning troops would be less than enthusiastic with prohibitionist sentiments at home. To forestall trouble in the U.S., Congress adopted wartime prohibition on November 21, 1918, to take effect on July 1, 1919, and to continue throughout the demobilization period.

During the war, Canadian distillery efforts had, like those in the U.S., been directed toward the production of industrial alcohol and bowing to public pressure. An order-in-council was passed on March 21, 1918, which became effective twenty-one days later. The order prohibited manufacture and importation of liquors containing more than 2.5 per cent alcohol until one year after the end of the war. A welcome loophole exempted alcohol for medicinal purposes. It goes to say that as a result, Canada sported the largest number of sick people it ever had, requiring a flood of prescriptions for whisky the like of which no country had ever seen before.

The only way to obtain whisky legally in the U.S. during the Prohibition era was to obtain a medical prescription for medicinal purposes.
(Author collection)

With the expiry of the order-in-council at the end of 1919, the House of Commons amended the Canada Temperance Act to continue Prohibition throughout the country, a move that was rejected by the Canadian Senate because of pressure exerted by Quebec, which had voted to legalize the sale of beer and wine in April of 1919.

By a compromise, the federal government agreed that the Canada Temperance Act should apply, after an order-in-council, to provinces that submitted the prohibition question to the voters and received popular support for the measures. In due course, most provinces approved the ban on alcohol, but it was not long before they acceded to pressure for the sale of liquor under provincial control.

Though it was banished from provinces other than Quebec, with the exception of the medicinal-purposes loophole, it has never been claimed that Canadians went without their alcohol. Conniving shipowners and captains, aided by a studied laxity on the part of customs officers, resulted in a widespread flaunting of the law. Politically appointed customs men were never anxious to cause waves that might cost jobs, and until the mid-1920s, drinkers would suffer little from lack of spirits.

Another contributing fact was that Canadian distilleries could produce alcohol for export purposes. This factor set the stage for the opening of the floodgates of the liquor traffic of the decade ahead.

In fact, distillers had export docks; a dory could come alongside the Hiram Walker wharf in Walkerville, Ontario, and load up twenty-five cases of Canadian Club whisky. A customs officer would stamp the customs clearance of the dory for Havana Cuba. This was rather a long row, and everyone was "officially amazed" to see the dory back shortly afterward looking for another load, as it had discharged in Havana, better known as Detroit, Michigan.

Liquor produced in Canada would be brought into the States by every imaginative way that could be thought of in order to keep the U.S. wet during the supposed dry period.

From the earliest of times, Newfoundlanders had made visits to the islands of St. Pierre and Miquelon, where well-stocked business establishments were only too happy to sell them goods. In St. Pierre, there was a well-organized merchant class with excellent stocks of liquor and tobacco at most attractive prices.

Rumrunning was a tradition in Newfoundland. In fact, it was of such proportions that Her Majesty's customs, in the person of Mr. James Hayward, visited St. Pierre in 1864 to get first-hand information on the magnitude of the traffic. According to reports he appeared to be such a nice, simple man that French Government officials in St. Pierre gave him every facility to acquire information. In the report that followed his visit, he stated that the Newfoundland revenue was robbed every year of about $50,000 due to smuggling of tobacco and alcohol from St. Pierre. Toward the end of the 1800s, the sum was said to be have escalated to more than double.

Newfoundlanders would bring over large quantities of herring that would be used by the French fishing fleet as bait. Hard pressed for cash, the barter system worked well. They would also bring firewood that was called, in those days, billets, spruce for making spruce beer, lamb, mussels, clams, knitted goods, and the like.

In the early part of the 1900s, Newfoundlanders from the south coast would barter billets (firewood), clams, mussels, and partridges for rum in St. Pierre.
(Photo courtesy of Briand-Ozon collection)

The islands of St. Pierre and Miquelon were a large outlet and the centre of an active business on Newfoundland's southwest coast. Here was collected together the merchandise offered both from France and America. There were large American-owned warehouses in the trade, such as Atherton Hughes and Robinson Export Co.

The contraband trade was so extensive that imports to St. Pierre amounted to over $480 per head, at least $450 of which was smuggled back into Newfoundland and Canada. The imports to Newfoundland at the same period in the 1800s were about $36.00 per head.

In 1887, the Newfoundland Government, seeking to protect the presence of the island's fishery, saw with satisfaction the controversial "Bait Bill" sanctioned by the British Government. The Act forbade the selling of bait to fishermen of foreign countries. This appeared to be aimed specifically at the French, since an agreement between Newfoundland and the United States already exempted American fishermen from its provision. Passage of the bill resulted in a heavy smuggling trade between Newfoundland and St. Pierre, despite heavy penalties for Newfoundlanders caught selling bait.

The legislators who had enacted the bait bill were disappointed that the ban failed to produce the desired effect, since resourceful St. Pierre fishermen turned to using shellfish such as clams, mussels, periwinkles, and other species that were not quite as satisfactory as herring or squid. The French fishermen were able to continue their fishing activities and prove that they could get along without bait from Newfoundland.

Nevertheless, the Bait Act was a serious blow to the commercial success of St. Pierre and, as a result, rumrunning diminished temporarily. Eventual relaxation a few years later brought back normality.

The First World War and its aftermath changed everything in the region. The Canada Temperance Act banned alcohol throughout Canada in 1919, and in the same year, France legislated an interdiction of the importation of foreign alcohol, including Demerara rum.

MCCOY DISCOVERS ST. PIERRE

The unwelcome – though not surprising – effect of the National Prohibition Act in the U.S. was the building of a multitude of illicit stills across the length and breadth of the nation.

The liquor produced from stills, strong and sometimes lethal, gave rise to a steady stream of reports of alcohol poisoning. It wasn't long before quiet bars, restaurants, and hotels sought sources for a reliable supply of good, imported liquor, and perceiving a market with substantial profits, there were those who soon sought to supply the demand.

One of those who quickly became interested in bringing the so-called good liquor from outside was a six-foot-two individual described as having shoulders like a cargo hatch, a slim waist, a voice like a foghorn, a lean, tanned face, and steady eyes. His name was Bill McCoy. McCoy was born in upper New York and as a youngster moved with his family to Florida.

After January 1919, Americans were begging for a drink. A friend of McCoy suggested that Nassau was a short sail away from Florida, and that the Bahamian Islands were filled with rum and whisky, with numerous merchants itching to sell it. The friend suggested to McCoy, who had graduated from navigational school, that he should take over as captain of his vessel. McCoy declined, as he didn't feel his friend's vessel was seaworthy.

Meanwhile, it had planted the seeds in McCoy that rumrunning was in its infancy and that it could be a good deal. There were millions of thirsty throats to be satisfied and there were thousands of cases of liquor in the Bahamas, with thousands more being hurried over from Europe. Ships able to make the trip to the American Coast were few. On the other hand, shipowners who could guarantee delivery of a cargo were even less plentiful.

Bill McCoy "The Real McCoy," centre, with shirt and tie, was the first American to place St. Pierre on the map as a supply base during Prohibition. (Photo courtesy of Mr. Joe Flemming)

McCoy decided to enter the trade on his own and went to Gloucester, Massachusetts, where he purchased the ninety-foot fishing schooner called the *Henry L. Marshall*.

In the early months of 1921, the *Marshall* sailed for Nassau, which was still a quiet little town, since the liquor trade was just at its beginning. Nassau assessed a duty of $6.00 per case on incoming liquor shipments.

Usually vessels would clear customs in Nassau or Halifax with the actual liquor shipments mentioned, then proceed to the west end of the Bahamas, where a complacent customs officer would issue duplicate customs clearance papers showing that the vessel was in ballast rather than loaded with whisky.

This became routine procedure whereby the west end official profited considerably, until complaints from the U.S. put a stop to the practice.

From then on, rumrunning vessels cleared for Halifax but never got there. When the vessels returned to Nassau, the captains signed an affidavit that he had sold his vessel's cargo on the high seas, and that he had made no stopovers in any other port. This satisfied the Nassau customs officials and became from then on the usual procedure.

The first trip undertaken by McCoy was to the coast of Georgia, where he successfully unloaded 1,500 cases of whisky on waiting launches. At $10.00 a case, he had banked $15,000, which wasn't bad for a week's work.

On her next voyage the *Marshall* went off to New York with another 1,500 cases of whisky. Thus McCoy can be credited as being the father of "Rum Row," the no man's land in international waters off New York, where a multitude of rumrunners would eventually unload their cargoes into smaller vessels that would then run them ashore.

The *Marshall* had been the first vessel to bring to New York such a large quantity of liquor. The idea of bringing liquor from the sea was a novel one, and no system had evolved to deal with it by the authorities. The Department of Justice had in fact made no particular preparations to handle violations of the Volstead Act.

McCoy was getting richer and richer by the day, and his customers were telling him much more liquor would be needed; they wanted him to purchase a larger vessel that could handle a minimum of 5,000 cases.

He followed that advice and started looking for a vessel. He settled on the *Arethusa*, a beautiful schooner that was tied up in Gloucester, as the fishing company that owned her had gone bankrupt.

He had to rename her *Tomoka*, as under British registry there was already another vessel by the name *Arethusa*.

McCoy felt that rumrunning was a "sporty enterprise." In this type of sport you could also lose, which is exactly what happened when his *Henry L. Marshall* was seized off Atlantic City, New Jersey, by the cutter *Seneca*.

Problems followed McCoy as a result of the confiscation of this vessel. The authorities found written sailing orders in the cabin signed by McCoy, as well as a set of double clearance papers. They were looking for him and he knew that he, and the *Tomoka* off

The schooner *Arethusa* was one of the pioneers on Rum Row during Prohibition. (Photo courtesy of the Marine Museum of the Atlantic, Halifax)

Bill McCoy's schooner *Arethusa* was renamed *Tomoka*.
(Photo courtesy of Mrs. Revert collection.)

Massachusetts, had to change position for a while. He ordered his captain to head for Halifax and wait outside the territorial waters for further instructions. The schooner also needed repairs.

McCoy immediately took a steamer from Boston to Yarmouth, Nova Scotia, and then proceeded to Halifax by rail.

Once in Halifax, McCoy visited the collector of customs, Mr. Bill Acker, and requested permission for his rumrunner to enter for repairs. This was denied as the schooner still had a fair number of cases of whisky in her hold.

In spite of McCoy's protests, pointing out she was a British-registered vessel with a British crew, there was nothing that could be done to change Acker's decision.

In the early 1920s, Halifax was too strict to have any dealings with rumrunners. At that stage, Nova Scotia was dryer than America.

McCoy ended up in the Carleton Hotel, where he was pacing the floor in the hotel's lobby. While doing this, there was another gentleman doing the same thing, and both men exchanged a few words. McCoy, realizing that the other gentleman had a French accent, spontaneously asked him where he was from in Quebec. He was told that he wasn't, but that he came from the French Islands of St. Pierre and Miquelon located off Newfoundland's south coast.

McCoy was astonished. He wasn't aware that France had a colony so close to Canadian soil.

McCoy informed his new-found friend, whose surname was Folquet, of the problems that he was encountering with his partially laden rumrunner, which badly needed repairs.

Folquet, an astute businessman with a twinkle in his eyes, told McCoy that he could send his vessel to St. Pierre for repairs where she could be dry docked on the marine railway, and that he and his schooner would be welcomed on the islands. He told him that his company, Folquet Brothers, were ships agents and could look after the vessel, and further advised him that if he wanted some French liquors for his trade, they would be only too willing to supply him at competitive prices. Likely there were products that were not available in Nassau.

The *Tomoka* set course for St. Pierre and upon arrival was taken in charge by the Folquets, who were distinguished businessmen on the little island. In McCoy's opinion, there were fair-dealing men in rumrunning, as you would encounter in any other business.

Foremost among all of these in honesty and trust, he placed the Folquet Brothers. This first visit was the beginning of a long friendship.

The *Tomoka* was the first rumrunning vessel to call in at the tiny island. McCoy was in effect the pioneer in opening up the liquor trade from that port. As a result of that visit by McCoy, St. Pierre was to become Nassau's chief rival in the liquor trade. In fact, St. Pierre would eventually outstrip Nassau in later years, due to the fact that rumrunning activities were being conducted decently and in order in St. Pierre. This was not always the case in Nassau; there was never any of the violence of boom town rivalry that Nassau saw.

McCoy was being made welcome by the whole of St. Pierre. His arrival to the island had sparked a lot of interest among the town merchants, who were well-aware of the huge market possibilities created by the American Prohibition. One of the visitors who became aware of McCoy's schooner was one of St. Pierre's leading merchants, Mr. C. P. Chartier. The latter, after having heard McCoy telling him of his rumrunning experience, as well as the possibilities offered by the rumrunning trade, neglected the fact that French laws made it impossible for islanders to import foreign liquor.

By a decree of July 8, 1919, the French Government had extended to all its colonies, and protectorates, except Tunisia and Morocco, an interdiction against importing sugar, molasses, and alcohol from foreign sources. These were postwar measures to save foreign exchange.

McCoy explained to the St. Pierre merchant that the dry Americans were chiefly interested in rye whisky, and unless the law could be changed, no substantial trade could readily exist.

Chartier and the other merchants, including Folquet Brothers, made it clear to McCoy that they would take the matter up with the French Government. These merchants had been amazed at Nassau's experience, and the prosperity that had come to the British colony in the few short months since it became involved in the liquor trade.

Success following the merchant's request came when the French Government made a special point of lifting this interdiction on April 18, 1922. St. Pierre was now open for business. All the rye and Scotch whisky could now come in. A small tax of about $0.40 would be charged on each case, which would finance local projects. This was considerably cheaper than Nassau's charges of $6.00 per case.

There was only one exception: rum from the British Guyana, which was prohibited so as to protect the producers from Guadeloupe and Martinique.

McCoy had not intentionally gone to St. Pierre as a rumrunning missionary. His sole purpose had been to find a dock on which his

Vintage French champagne of 1914 being unloaded in St. Pierre, circa 1922, to be reshipped to the American Coast. (Photo courtesy of Mrs. Y. Andrieux collection)

White Horse Scotch Whisky being unloaded in St. Pierre, circa 1922.
(Photo courtesy of Mrs. Y. Andrieux collection)

Top and bottom: Shipment of champagne being unloaded during Prohibition, circa 1922. (Photo courtesy of Mrs. Y. Andrieux collection)

vessel could get her repairs. By chance, he had opened up a totally new venue in the rumrunning game. McCoy had put St. Pierre on the map.

McCoy became a legend in the trade, as he always dealt in first-class alcoholic products. His satisfied customers would say when you bought from McCoy, you got "the real McCoy," still today a byword for the genuine article and high quality.

In spite of the fact that St. Pierre opened up, McCoy still went to Nassau once in a while. Here he ended up with an unusual experience. He brought on the *Tomoka* the only woman who had come up thus far to "Rum Row" to sell her own liquor.

Gertrude Light was described by McCoy as being a tall, slender woman of barely thirty, with black hair and a brain as steady as her own dark eyes. She had come to Nassau as agent for a Scotch whisky Company. Nassau was not the best place in those days for an attractive, unprotected woman. Members of the rum mob had drawn their own conclusions concerning her, and had then tried to operate accordingly. She reacted with breathtaking speed and a couple of them ended up with a pistol jammed into their ribs by way of making things clear. She was an able and thoroughly competent person.

Light's firm in England had sent her over 1,000 cases of American bourbon, but had bottled it in fifths instead of quarts and could find no market on Rum Row for it. She called McCoy into her office one day and asked him to take her bourbon north. He refused, but each day thereafter she approached him with a new argument, and in course she nearly ran him ragged. She was a good business-woman and finally persuaded McCoy to take the shipment on deck. It being the summer, there was little danger of it being washed over-board if it were properly secured.

To McCoy's great surprise, as the schooner was ready to sail, she announced that she was going on board, in order to look after her cargo. McCoy didn't want her aboard, and warned her that it would be a rough trip and that most of the crew were a rough gang. It was an empty argument, as she would go to Rum Row with them whether McCoy wished to or not.

Her first act in settling in on the voyage was to have a .38 Colt and holster placed inside her bunk.

The effect of a woman's presence aboard a rumrunner was laughable. The rest of the crew were a bit shy in her presence and hung back a little, except the cook, who McCoy had nicknamed "Frenchy Revert." He had joined the schooner when McCoy had made his historic first voyage to St. Pierre. On his native island he was affectionately known as "Lapin Revert," for as a "rabbit" he was not shy, approaching her at once with a prance in his gait as he launched into an oration on the good things he intended to cook for her, and the music he would play on his violin whenever she wished.

A list of liquor cases being loaded at St. Pierre on various rumrunning vessels.
(Document courtesy of Mr. A. Bechet)

The crew liked her from the beginning and, because of her presence, the rumrunner was cleaned up like a yacht. The men actually brushed their hair, put on clean clothes, and the cook put on a new apron.

Fair weather accompanied them to Rum Row and they were able to eat on the afterdeck every day.

The cook outdid himself, and prepared new and amazing dishes unlike any he had ever served before. In the evenings the crew would come aft and the cook would play his violin or his accordion and they would all sing sea shanties. With Gertrude Light on board, the *Tomoka*'s crew on deck behaved more like a crowd attending a Sunday school picnic rather than a group of rumrunners.

Gertrude Light's presence paid off. Upon arriving at Rum Row, McCoy was able to sell her goods over the side, to her great satisfaction. Other schooners were sailing back to Nassau, so she transferred aboard for the return trip. As she was anxious to return, off she went.

She had just accomplished a trip to Rum Row that very few women would ever duplicate.

THE WHISKY FLOOD COMMENCES

The ban to import foreign liquor having been lifted, the SS *Sable Island*, owned by Farquhar Line, docked in St. Pierre on July 8, 1922, with a cargo of 12,000 cases of Canadian Club rye whisky. It marked the beginning of the most frantic period of activity the colony had ever seen. It was an event that transformed the island and profoundly affected the lives of its people.

Before the advent of the liquor traffic, St. Pierre had for some years been a quiet fishing village, suffering from economic recession. There were high hopes among the islanders that the lifting of the interdiction against the import of foreign alcohol might somehow improve prospects for jobs, but no one could dream of the degree or dimensions of commerce that unfolded. News of McCoy's first visit to the islands had spread like wildfire through the liquor circles. It was ironic that the Morue Francaise, the local company that controlled the fish business, bank, stores, warehouses, bakery, freight vessels, the government mail contract, and other enterprises, was sluggish to react.

They were well-financed and had all the connections and resources to take full advantage of this new bonanza. However, top management was at head office in Paris, and this distance from the scene of action contributed heavily in the company's failure to realize the implications of Prohibition and the resultant opportunities for business in St. Pierre.

While the Morue Francaise had not reacted, C. P. Chartier, who

28

had been a visitor on McCoy's schooner, and who had persuaded the government to remove the interdiction to import foreign alcohol, lost no time. He formed a partnership with Montreal interests in a firm called the St. George Import and Export Co. Chartier's associates were members of the George family, who acted as export agents for Hiram Walker-Gooderham & Worts Ltd., of Walkerville, Ontario.

The first shipment of Hiram Walker products on the SS *Sable Island* consigned to C. P. Chartier signalled the beginning of the St. George firm's activities. Two sailing vessels from Glasgow, Scotland, arrived in October. The *Anne Antoinette* and *La Flaneuse* each brought 6,000 cases of White Horse Scotch Whisky. The *Sable Island* returned on December 9, with a further 12,000 cases of rye whisky, and nine days later the three-master *Yvonne* arrived from Scotland with an additional 6,500 cases of Scotch.

These cargoes caused a sensation, to say nothing about creating

The *Sable Island*, owned by Farquhar Steamships of Halifax, was the first vessel to bring in a load of Canadian whisky to St. Pierre during the Prohibition era. (Photo courtesy of Mrs. Y. Andrieux collection)

an instant warehousing crisis. As a result, every available basement was rented to store liquor. Fishermen quickly abandoned their traditional occupation and overnight became stevedores, warehousemen, and cargo operators.

To describe what happened as a boom would be an understatement in this little fishing community.

The following year, 1923, more than 500,000 cases of liquor poured into the island. About 1,000 cargo or rumrunning vessels called in at the island. It was a volume of traffic never before imagined.

Initially, schooners would take the merchandise off to the American Coast where they would stay in international waters off Fire Island, New York. These waters became known as Rum Row. Small, fast shore vessels would come and load up, and then make their way to shore, hopefully without getting caught.

Criminal elements quickly acquired control of the flow of liquor in New York, dictated distribution and sale, financed nightclubs, and operated syndicates. It had liquor and other business-interest alliances which became countrywide.

The most negative and vicious development as a result of Prohibition was the strengthening of the criminal underworld. This was the element which in large part eventually controlled the great inflow of liquor from the sea, which was to become one of the greatest problems of the period and the particular concern of the U.S. Coast Guard.

The entire smuggling operation, from importation to final dispensing, was largely controlled by organized gangsters. Large sums of money were expended for the most modern and efficient equipment to defeat the Coast Guard and other enforcement agencies.

Smuggling of liquor took place all along the Atlantic and Gulf coasts. There were five principal points where entry by sea was chiefly concentrated. The largest and most important area was the New York area, including Long Island and New Jersey. It was in these waters that "Rum Row" had been established. A subsidiary Rum Row was also established off Boston.

There were two distinct operations out of St. Pierre: one to the U.S. Coast, primarily interested in importing rye and bourbon whisky, and a smaller amount of rye and bourbon went to Canada and Newfoundland, representing only about ten per cent of the market.

The Canadian and Newfoundland market was markedly different. The English-speaking areas wanted Demerara rum, while the French-speaking regions of New Brunswick and Quebec wanted the pure white alcohol, ninety-five per cent pure, that was known as Whisky Blanc, St. Pierre–Miquelon Whisky, or Hand Brand.

Demerara rum was not legally available on the island of St. Pierre. The French Government had banned its import in the colony in order to protect sales of rum from the French Caribbean.

This ban, coupled with the Eighteenth Amendment, created an excellent opportunity for Newfoundland vessels to become implicated in the rumrunning trade.

Demerara rum was said to have a taste and flavour of its own, and its potency was indefinable. The brand that was most in demand was Black Diamond, distilled by a company called Sandbach Parker of Georgetown, Demerara.

Newfoundland schooners of every type made the voyage to British Guyana. On their way down they would usually stop in Nova Scotian ports, where they would load up on purchases of five- and ten-gallon puncheons which

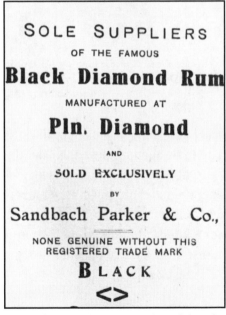

SOLE SUPPLIERS

OF THE FAMOUS

Black Diamond Rum

MANUFACTURED AT

Pln. Diamond

AND

SOLD EXCLUSIVELY

BY

Sandbach Parker & Co.,

NONE GENUINE WITHOUT THIS
REGISTERED TRADE MARK

B L A C K

<>

Black Diamond rum, produced by the Sandbach Parker distillery in Demerara, Guyana, was the most sought-after rum in Newfoundland and the Maritimes during the rumrunning era. (Document courtesy of Mr. Henri Moraze)

The *Standard Coaster* loading up empty barrels in Nova Scotia for a trip to Demerara in British Guyana to pick up Black Diamond rum.
(Photo courtesy of Captain R. C. Butt)

had been transported there in railroad cars from Waterloo, Ontario. The manufacturer was the Canada Barrel Co.

Once loaded, the vessel would proceed to Guyana to an anchorage where the empty barrels would be transferred to lighters and taken up to the distillery to be filled. Once that process was completed, the now filled five- and ten-gallon puncheons would be transferred back aboard the vessel and make their way back up the Atlantic Coast.

The favourite transfer point was the Burgeo Bank, in international waters. The rum would be transferred to smaller vessels and would be taken to various Newfoundland communities or up to Cape Breton, Nova Scotia, or to Prince Edward Island. Other lots made their way to bonded warehouses in St. John's where the rum would be kept in storage. One of the popular warehouses for storing rum was the Eastern Trading Co. Ltd.

The popularity of this rum attracted bigger operators, and they eventually dominated the Demerara trade. Names like Fudge, Petite, Ryan, and Kearley were household names in the business.

Captain Fudge operated the *Chappel Point*. She had a capacity to load 65,000 gallons per trip. The Petite firm operated the *Jean M. Wakely*, while Captain Ryan had the three-master *Russel M. Zinc*.

Negotiations were usually carried out in the early part of the year. For example, an order was placed in January for 6,000 gallons of Black Diamond rum at $2.00 per gallon. This included every-thing: barrels, freight, and contents. This was to be carried as a part-load on Captain Fudge's *Chappel Point*.

A vessel like the *Chappel Point* would take about fifteen days to make the voyage down.

Such stocks would eventually be cleared for the high seas and end up in Newfoundland outports or the Maritimes.

In the 1800s and early 1900s, prior to British Guyana rum being available, the Newfoundlanders would purchase French Caribbean rum.

This rum usually came in from Martinique and Guadeloupe by returning three-masters that had gone down with dried salt cod. It came up in large puncheons and would be bottled locally by St. Pierre merchants.

Other rum of inferior quality was made up in St. Pierre by mixing up a certain amount of genuine strong rum with molasses, pure white alcohol, water, and caramel colouring. This was cheap but not the best.

Some of the Newfoundland buyers were not particularly fond of this variety.

One wrote to one of his St. Pierre suppliers as follows:

> "Would prefer a Demerara rum but I don't want French alcohol coloured up. It would only spoil my trade. 1st lot would kill it all, so make no mistake about that. I want some standard brand. By standard brand I don't mean some queer rum one never heard

Top and bottom: Canadian whisky being taken to warehouses on St. Pierre.
(Photo courtesy of Mrs. Y. Andrieux collection)

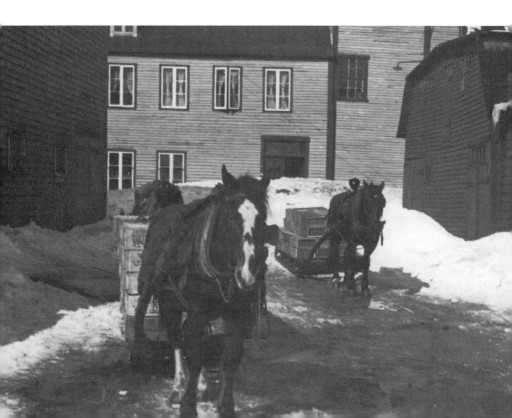

tell of, but something like Black Diamond. That's as long as you're not manufacturing it and bottling it yourself. Queer that you people down there don't keep a decent rum. You can buy it right, but I'm dammed if one can get a decent drink of rum in St. Pierre, and rum is one thing that can't be imitated. Any amateur can tell a good drink of rum from that rotgut they sell down there. I am afraid you fellows want to make too much money."

Norwegian vessels transported Scotch whisky from Scotland to St. Pierre. (Photo courtesy of Mrs. Y. Andrieux collection)

A busy waterfront scene as Scotch whisky is being unloaded and then transported to St. Pierre warehouses. (Photo courtesy of Mrs. Y. Andrieux collection)

Gaelic brand Scotch whisky being unloaded from a Norwegian flag freighter on St. Pierre. (Photo courtesy of Mrs. Y. Andrieux collection)

Workers with a case of Gaelic Scotch at the door of a St. Pierre liquor warehouse during the Prohibition era. (Photo courtesy of Mr. E. Lefevre)

Canadian Club whisky being loaded on a rumrunner in St. Pierre.
(Photo courtesy of Mrs. Y. Andrieux collection)

Contents of barrels of whisky were poured in giant funnels at St. Pierre on board banana boats (small tankers) that would off-load it by hose in small coves on the American Coast. (Photo courtesy of the Yarmouth County Historical Society's Museum and Research Library, Yarmouth, Nova Scotia)

Top and bottom: A load of bagged whisky being loaded on a rumrunner at St. Pierre during the Prohibition era. (Photo courtesy of the Yarmouth County Historical Society's Museum and Research Library, Yarmouth, Nova Scotia)

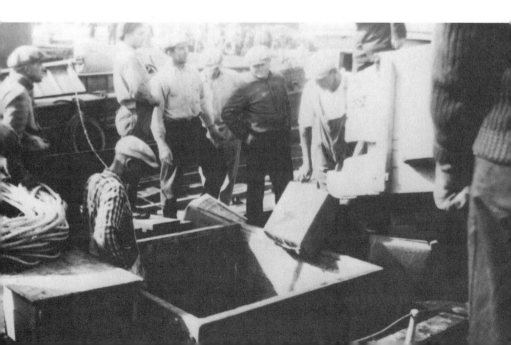

The schooner *Jean M. Wakely*, owned by Petite's of English Harbour West, would pick up loads of rum in British Guyana for resale.
(Photo courtesy of Captain H. W. Stone)

The schooner *Russel M. Zinc*, owned by Captain A. Ryan, loaded with Black Diamond rum awaiting for customers on the Burgeo Bank.
(Photo courtesy of Captain Milton MacKenzie)

Empty barrels being loaded for Demerara, Guyana, on a standard coaster rumrunner at a Nova Scotia port. Once there they would be filled up at the distillery and would be transferred to smaller vessels on the Burgeo Bank.

(Photo courtesy of Captain R. C. Butt)

Barrels of rum awaiting shipment on the docks of Demerara, British Guyana.

(Photo courtesy of Captain R. C. Butt)

A lighter being loaded with rum barrels to be delivered to a rumrunner at anchor at Demerara, British Guyana. (Photo courtesy of Captain R. C. Butt)

Rumrunning schooner *Charles L.*, owned by Petite's of English Harbour West, NL. (Photo courtesy of Captain R. C. Butt)

Whisky brands produced by Canadian distilleries for the American market during the Prohibition era. (Author collection)

John J. Bradley was one of the early foreign liquor distributors to establish a sales office on St. Pierre during the Prohibition era.
(Photo courtesy of Briand-Ozon collection)

CANADIAN DISTILLERS AND
THEIR SALES AGENTS

In the initial years of the Prohibition period, Canadian distillers were busy on many fronts, and were satisfied to sell to St. Pierre merchants or to forward shipments on a consignment basis.

One exception was a small Montreal distillery owned by John J. Bradley. This firm opened for business early in 1923 in St. Pierre as John J. Bradley Limited, importing and selling some of their own products as well as Scotch whisky and other liquor from abroad. The local manager was a Mr. Enslow. Bradley also had a sales agency in Saint John, New Brunswick. The operation lasted only about three years, ending with the death of its owner.

Because of the parliamentary committee's investigation and the Judicial Commission of 1926, distillers found it much more difficult to do business from Canada to U.S. points. Most of the principal distillers opened their own sales agencies in St. Pierre, the preferred foreign destination. However, in time, Montreal offices handled the transactions with American rumrunners, ordering shipments from St. Pierre warehouses.

In addition to the Canadian traders, some agencies were established by foreign interests. One such was Atlantic Trading Co., operated by R. B. Stevens, a Scot who had arrived in St. Pierre to act as agent for overseas distilleries; his principal product handled was Star Brand Alcohol.

Consolidated Exporters rented space in St. Pierre for its biggest-selling product, Guggenheim's Whisky. The firm had been formed in

Vancouver in 1922 by a group of liquor merchants, and its first manager in St. Pierre was a Mr. Halter. The company acted as agent for United Distillers of Vancouver.

United Distillers Limited was a large distillery from British Columbia that would ship products to St. Pierre during the Prohibition era.
(Document courtesy of Mr. Henri Moraze)

Consolidated Traders Co. was the sales agency of Consolidated Distilleries Ltd., with head office in Montreal. In turn, Consolidated Distilleries was a subsidiary of Canadian Industrial Alcohol Ltd. and had been set up to handle the export sales of various distilleries owned by the parent holding company.

One of the distilleries held by Canadian Industrial Alcohol was Corby's, of Belleville, Ontario. Acquired in 1918, this distilling operation had followed a pattern in its early years similar to that of other such enterprises. Many Canadian distilleries had their beginnings with immigrant families with a background in the grain business, a grist and flour milling operation with distilling as a subsidiary enterprise that eventually swallowed up all other interests.

Henry Corby began as a miller in Belleville in 1857, the distillery starting two years later. After his death in 1881, his son Harry headed the enterprise until 1907. During the twenty-six-year period he was in charge, a great expansion took place. He was a highly competent merchandiser and executive and the name Corby became one of the leaders in Canadian whisky.

At age sixty, Harry Corby sold his interests to a younger man, Mortimer Davis (Sir Mortimer after 1917), who had been with the company for two years. The firm was then incorporated as H. Corby Distilleries Co. Ltd., and extended its business into the American market, continuing the connection begun by Harry Corby with imported wines and Scotch whisky.

The Corby distillery was razed by a great fire in 1907, and rebuilt on even larger lines. Whisky making was discontinued during World War I, and in 1918 Corby's became part of Canadian Industrial Alcohol, of Montreal.

Corby's distillery in Ontario. (Photo courtesy of the RCMP Archives)

Harry Hatch was Corby's sales manager. Hatch had begun his association with the liquor industry as a small hotel owner; he then joined Corby's and moved upward through the various stages of the business until he became assistant to the president of the parent company, Canadian Industrial Alcohol. In 1923, with associates, Harry Hatch bought the long-established Gooderham & Worts distillery of Toronto, becoming president. Three years later, Hiram Walker's Distillery, of Walkerville, was added, and the business reestablished as Hiram Walker-Gooderham & Worts Limited.

In St. Pierre, Consolidated Traders Co. opened offices in the J. B. Legasse building and rented warehouses. The first manager was a Mr. Rose, sent to set up the business, followed soon by Rod Sutherland. In 1930, Louis Ozon was manager. Most popular of their whiskies was "William Penn." The company also acted as agent for many European distilleries and distributed Cutty Sark Scotch, Gilbey's products, and numerous others.

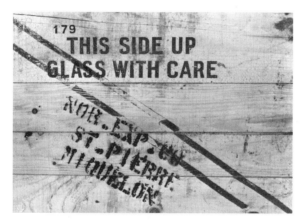

A case of whisky addressed to Northern Export Company in St. Pierre. This company was owned by the Bronfman family of Montreal. (Author collection)

The Great West Wine Co. was a sales agency created to distribute the products of the British Columbia Distillery, of New Westminster, British Columbia. The distillery, in turn, was owned by a holding company, Brewers and Distillers of Vancouver Ltd., which also controlled two breweries in Vancouver, one in Victoria, one in Nanaimo, and a distillery in Amherstburg, Ontario. A substantial percentage of the holding company was owned in Britain. George W. Twittey had come from there to assume the post of secretary-treasurer. Another Briton named Howatson had arrived at the same time and was manager of the company. The president was Henry Reifel, a German immigrant who settled in British Columbia in the late 1880s.

Great West's office in St. Pierre was represented by a local manager, Louis Hardy, and the firm's largest-selling brand was Four Aces whisky.

The parent organization had been very active during Prohibition; after Repeal, the U.S. Government charged Canadian distilleries with involvement in smuggling and made strenuous efforts to make good its claim to unpaid taxes. In the case of the Vancouver firm, Reifel was in the limelight to the extent that British shareholders forced him to divest himself of his interests. He was followed as president by Col. Henry S. Tobin. The two distilleries were later sold to Bronfman interests, the breweries to Canadian Breweries, later known as Carling-O'Keefe, and eventually merged with the Molson interests.

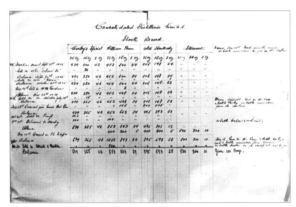

An inventory list of stocks owned by Consolidated Distilleries warehoused in St. Pierre. (Photo courtesy of Mr. Henri Moraze)

The Island Liquor Co. was operated by the Yule brothers, brothers-in-law of the owners of the Lindsay Distillery in Lindsay, Ontario. The latter was a small operation by comparison with the large distilleries that dominated the trade. Principal brands of Lindsay were "Saratoga" and "Cedar Brook" whiskies. Lindsay Distilleries ceased operation in 1932.

Pre-eminent among the traders in St. Pierre was Northern

Export Company, the distribution arm of the Bronfman interests on the island. The full story of the Bronfmans has been told in detail in two excellent books: *Booze*, by James H. Gray, New American Library of Canada, 1972; and *The Bronfman Dynasty*, Peter C. Newman, McLelland & Stewart Ltd., Toronto, 1978.

Yechiel and Minnie Bronfman, with their three children, had fled their native Bessarabia during the pogroms and emigrated to Western Canada. In time, one of the elder sons, Harry, acquired the Balmoral Hotel in Yorkton, Saskatchewan, and began to lay the foundations of the family fortune. Other sons added more hotels, and after the end of World War I they became involved in the liquor business in Western Canada. In 1919, there was a huge surplus of whisky in Scotland, a time when the product was in short supply in Canada, since Canadian distilleries had been converted for the production of industrial alcohol needed for war purposes. Harry Bronfman acquired a bonded warehouse licence in Yorkton and began importing Scotch by the railway carload. Through a quirk in the liquor laws, over a thirty-month period it was legal to send whisky by mail from one province for consumption in another, and the Bronfmans took full advantage of this oddity. In due time, to maximize profits, Harry Bronfman began importing Scotch in bulk, with blending and bottling carried on in Yorkton, and later Regina.

Changing times and the inception of provincial liquor commissions put an end to this phase of the business, but led to the supplying of the international bootlegging trade by automobile across the forty-ninth parallel. Another development was the building, in LaSalle, Quebec, of a distillery that became one of the world's largest. Operations there commenced in 1924.

As well as the products from LaSalle, whiskies were supplied from other distilleries. One of these was Highland Scotch Distilleries, of Humberstone, Ontario, now part of Port Colborne. The buildings were located on Killaly Street East, by the Lake Erie end of the Welland Canal, across the lake from Buffalo, New York. The first housed three offices in front, wooden vats in the centre, and the boiler room in the rear. The second held the wooden barrels of whisky for aging, with bottling supplies in the third structure. Raw, syrupy-thick whisky arrived in Humberstone, where each barrel was cut by adding two barrels of distilled water. This was pumped to the third building into copper tanks where it was bottled, wrapped, labelled, packed into sacks, and finally placed in boxes for storage in the warehouse. Products included Babbling Brook Bourbon Whisky, and Goodwill Pure Rye Whisky, bottled in sixteen-ounce flasks and three-cornered bottles holding twenty-six and forty ounces. The operation was controlled from Montreal, and Sam Bronfman made frequent visits to Humberstone.

In 1926, the Bronfmans sold a half-interest in their LaSalle distillery to the giant Distillers Corporation, of Britain. Among Distillers Corporation's most popular products were Vat 69, Dewar's, White Horse, Black and White, Johnnie Walker, Gordon's Dry Gin, Tanqueray, and others. In Canada, the Distillers Corporation acquired, a year later, the prestigious Seagram Distillery in Waterloo, Ontario. Seagram's had been established in 1857; its roots were deep in the prosperous Ontario countryside and its reputation first-class in every respect.

Old Dougherty bottle used by Canadian distillers for the American market. (Author collection)

In the latter part of 1927, the Bronfmans set up their own sales agency in St. Pierre, Northern Export Company. Monte Rosebourne was sent to the island to manage the operation. Soon after opening for business, Northern Export acquired Bill Miller's St. Pierre Distributing Company. Within months, Northern Export had become St. Pierre's largest trader.

By March 1931, the major Canadian distilleries agreed to

organize a "pool" in the interests of higher profits through lessened competition. Northern Export joined forces with the largest independent dealer in St. Pierre, C. P. Chartier, and Rosebourne headed the pool, moving into Chartier's office building. Participation of each distillery in the pool was as follows: Distillers Corporation, thirty-eight per cent; Consolidated Distillers, nineteen per cent; British Columbia Distilleries, eight per cent; United Distillers, eight per cent; and Hiram Walker, twenty-seven per cent.

The pool purchased supplies from member distillers and their agencies, as well as products from small independent distilleries. The arrangement lasted only a few months, Walker's apparently losing interest in the pool plan.

The distillers made most of their sales to the bootlegger and smuggling trade. Visits would be made to Montreal offices, followed by telegrams to St. Pierre giving the breakdown of quantities to be loaded on rumrunners' vessels. Sales also would take place in St. Pierre directly with rumrunners who arrived on their own, as well as to the merchants of St. Pierre and Miquelon.

At its height, Northern Export's staff comprised some seventy employees in the office and warehouses, all locally recruited except for the manager.

The only French company involved in the trade in St. Pierre was the Societe d'Importation et d'Exportation (SIE). It was controlled by the giant Morue Francaise interests and acted as agent for a number of brands of French champagne, Scotch whisky, rye whisky, and other products. However, in comparison to the large Canadian distilleries, its percentage of the total sales was modest. They owned their own warehouses in St. Pierre.

United Traders Co. distributed Walker's products. The company operated out of the Morue Francaise warehouses, where space was leased, and several thousand cases of Canadian Club whisky were always on hand. The company registered in Nassau, Bahamas, with Bill Hull as manager in St. Pierre. A suite of offices was maintained at the Mount Royal Hotel, Montreal, where American buyers would place their orders. Walker's never opened sales offices in St. Pierre in their own name. During the first few years, distribution of Walker's whiskies had been a function of the George interests of Montreal. This was the St. George Import and Export Co., in partnership with local St. Pierre merchant C. P. Chartier. When the latter operation closed, United Traders became distributors of the Walker line.

Generally in St. Pierre, as the years passed and the smuggling trade changed, with refinements both by the boatmen and the Preventive Service officers, the business was taken over by few agencies, thoroughly financed with the most modern communications at their disposal. It was very big business indeed; during the Prohibition period the United States Coast Guard was estimated to have seized 1,300 boats presumed to have been in the trade. Many of these were well-known in St. Pierre and Miquelon.

Distillers Corporation distillery in LaSalle, QC. (Author collection)

Consolidated Traders office in St. Pierre during the Prohibition era. This was owned by Consolidated Distilleries of Montreal. (Photo courtesy of Mr. Marcel Girardin)

St. Pierre entrepreneurs built large warehouses that would be rented to Canadian distillers to stow their products during the Prohibition era. (Photo courtesy of Mr. Clem Cusick)

J. B. Legasse was representative in St. Pierre of Melcher's Distilleries from Berthierville, QC. On the left is rumrunning vessel *Corticelli* waiting for its load.
(Photo courtesy of Briand-Ozon collection)

Rumrunners being loaded in St. Pierre.
(Photo courtesy of Briand-Ozon collection)

A warehouse built by Henri Moraze in St. Pierre and rented to Northern Export during the Prohibition era. (Photo courtesy of Briand-Ozon collection)

A large schooner unloading onto a fast rumrunner in international waters.
(Photo courtesy of Captain R. C. Butt)

A rumrunner at sea.
(Photo courtesy of Captain R. C. Butt)

DIMENSIONS OF THE LIQUOR TRADE

When the major distillers set up shop in St. Pierre, they completely changed the distribution and marketing patterns for liquor during the Prohibition period. They monopolized the market.

Canadian products held the major share. Representatives of the distilleries were sent to scour European producers for exclusive distribution rights. The St. Pierre merchants generally had insufficient capital to be able to deal with a trade aimed at supplying a large portion of the huge American and Canadian markets. If a St. Pierre man was able to purchase 5,000 cases of a distiller's product, a big Canadian firm would propose a 50,000-case order to achieve its goal.

In the latter years of Prohibition, the import pattern on the French Islands saw the trade fall into constantly fewer hands. The breakdown was as follows: Northern Export Co., sixty per cent; Consolidated Exporters Ltd., ten per cent; Consolidated Traders Co., ten per cent; Great West Wine Co., ten per cent; United Traders Co., five per cent; all others, five per cent. Thus, ninety-five per cent of all import activities were controlled by the Canadian distillers themselves.

St. Pierre merchants, initially in charge of all the business, were relegated to the role of jobbers. They would purchase from distillers or their agents at a discounted price and sell to their customers at the going tariff. But the bulk of the transactions were consummated in Montreal, where the big companies had offices in the downtown area, to deal with Americans who made their purchases there.

Payment was usually in cash; a letter or telegram would be sent to St. Pierre authorizing the release of goods to a rumrunning vessel.

Where American customers had connections among the independent merchants, there was some trade directly with St. Pierre. On some occasions the local men extended credit, unavailable through the big distilleries. Though payments were often made in St. Pierre, in sum total they were small compared with the total volume generated by the trade. Most banking was done through the St. Pierre branch of the Canadian Bank of Commerce.

With the eventual tightening of inspections and plugging of loopholes, it became increasingly difficult for liquor to enter the United States. Ingenuity and imagination were needed and successfully employed, to market whisky and other liquors and wines and to assure their safe arrival to the consumer.

A RUMRUNNING STORY

A small vessel from Newfoundland arrived in St. Pierre and loaded 500 small barrels of whisky. The fishing vessel brought with it a cargo of herring. The kegs of whisky were fitted into the larger herring barrels and the schooner cleared for a port on the east coast of Newfoundland, loading pickled herring to completely conceal the whisky. Next stop was St. John's, where the "herring" was discharged for furtherance to New York aboard the *Nerissa* of the Red Cross Line. All went smoothly and the cargo left St. John's without suspicion having been aroused. Unfortunately, when the *Nerissa* was being discharged in New York, careless handling resulted in a "herring" barrel falling from a sling and crashing to the ground. The scheme was discovered and the entire shipment confiscated.

Many of the men who crewed rumrunners came from Lunenburg, Nova Scotia. Two views on rumrunning prevailed in Lunenburg; the stakes were high, there was money to be made, but lives could also be lost in the trade. For the most part, it was the middleman who suffered in playing what became an increasingly dangerous game and way of life. However, during the Depression years, many were tempted to earn a livelihood in the rumrunning vessels. Lunenburg men served on both sides of the law; while many crewed the rumrunners, others served in the Coast Guard, whose mission it was to intercept them.

Records show the Canadian distillers with a fleet of eighty or more carriers available on call to deliver whisky to U.S. and Canadian points. In 1933, for instance, the following vessels were operating out of St. Pierre:

Administratix, Achalaunza, Amaioitia, Afachauk, Anna D, Alva, Atacama, Annett S, Arnaldo York, Accuracy, Arco, Betty & Ida, Bambi, Bettina, Barbara, Baronet, Bearcat, Bath, Cassie Belle, Connoisseur, Corticelli, Diana, Diamantina, Dorin, Etchepotchi, Fly, Fannie May, Golmacoan, Galiano, Gertrude Jean, Good Luck, Grace Marie, George and Earl, Henry Djo, Isabel H, Ida, Josephine K, Kromhout, La Sirene, Lida, Lomergrain, Mabel, Malbo, Marelton, Margaret H, Margaret S II, Marie Yvonne, Marion B, Mary B, Mary F, Ruth, Matilda C, May B, May and June, Mazeltov, Miralda, Miserinko, Mudathalapadu, Narmada, Nell, Nellie J, Banks, Nova V, Olga, Owl, Pronto, Popocatapelt, Radio I, Red Rose, Selma K, Schvatka, Schanalian, Thomas and Robert, Telio, Upsalquitch, Vanaheim, Winoma R, and Yamaska.

These vessels operated during the period of the month when there was no moon, so they couldn't be noticed unloading their cargo during the night. Huge quantities were being handled from the island. At its height, up to 350,000 cases a month were being shipped.

The rumrunning vessels faced one major problem. The liquor was packed in wooden cases. When the cases were being transferred off the American Coast, it made a considerable noise. Even though it could be a dark, moonless night, the Coast Guard cutters were standing by and could hear this noise, which resulted in the occasional arrest of one of the rumrunners.

The *Mary Pauline* was used in rumrunning operations to the U.S. Coast. She was ultimately lost with all her crew except one in a winter storm off St. Pierre in December 1963. (Photo courtesy of Mr. Alex Hardy)

Rumrunning schooner *St. Pierraise* on Newfoundland's northeast coast, 1933, delivering alcohol to small outports of the region.
(Photo courtesy of Mrs. Marie Enguehard)

A well-dressed customer off Jackson's Arm awaiting delivery of a small pun-
cheon of rum while a young man holds a bottle of spirits.
(Photo courtesy of Mrs. Marie Enguehard)

Rumrunning schooner *St. Pierraise* tied up at wharf in Hooping Harbour, White
Bay, NL, 1933. (Photo courtesy of Mrs. Marie Enguehard)

CAPONE LEAVES A SOUVENIR

St. Pierre's prominence in the liquor business during Prohibition attracted plenty of curiosity in the world of speakeasy operators, consumers who inquired about the source of their liquid solace, and those involved in attempting to put a stop to the trade.

Among the latter was the captain of a Preventive Service cutter, known to his crew, without affection, as "Old Goosey." An avid tee-totaller, his consuming interest in life was to catch as many rumrunners as possible. When he anchored his vessel in the outer harbour of St. Pierre, his mission was to satisfy his curiosity about the starting point for those he was dedicated to laying by their heels.

Old Goosey planned a trip ashore to observe the warehousing operations, but it was to be a solo visit. He mistrusted his crew, lest they become tempted to sample the best-known St. Pierre products, and ordered them to remain aboard.

His fears were soundly based. In those times, a visitor to any of the local liquor merchants would find a row of kegs at the rear of the shop from which one could sample the goods. Crews of visiting vessels were familiar with the hospitality and indulged freely; they found that generous quantities of the best available were guaranteed to relieve anxieties about forthcoming voyages to American waters infested with Coast Guard ships and gangster-owned boats bent on hijacks.

Goosey had an invitation to visit the governor of St. Pierre, and he left on his mission in one of his ship's lifeboats, with strict orders to his executive officer not to allow any of the crew off the vessel.

Fog is a feature of the weather in St. Pierre, and shortly after the lifeboat's departure, a heavy blanket settled over the scene. The men who had brought Goosey ashore waited at dockside for his return. With time on their hands, they explored the harbourfront and soon came across the liquor warehouses, where delights of many varieties were readily available. In short order they purchased some forty cases of mixed products for a modest sum and promptly returned with it to the cutter.

What to do with their treasure was a problem. Willing hands settled the issue by opening a manhole cover and emptying the liquor into a water tank. An indiscriminate mixture of champagne, Benedictine, and rye instantly created what was probably the world's greatest cocktail.

Unhappily for them, as they were pulling away from the St. Pierre dock with the last of their cases, they came under the eye of a couple of French gendarmes, on patrol. The word, in due course, was relayed to Goosey, who indignantly denied that any of his enforcement crew could be guilty of such conduct. To reinforce his point, he invited the French police aboard to see for themselves. A search of the vessel revealed nothing.

Next morning, as the cutter prepared to leave St. Pierre, the captain had a superbly drunken crew on his hands. Minute searches of the ship failed to reveal the source of the debacle, though the master, had he noted the number of visits to a certain water tap by his inebriated crewmen, might have twigged to the source of his troubles. Goosey searched high and low, from mast to keel, over a period of three or four days during which he had to station an officer at the wheel, as the crew remained blissfully *hors de combat*. Finally, on the last day of his combing of every nook and cranny, Goosey emerged from the engine room, covered with soot and grime – and thirsty. One turn of the water faucet and his search ended. He ordered the draining of the tank, to little avail; so diligent had his crew been, and so appreciative of the restorative and numbing effects of their cocktail, that the tank was by now almost dry.

If anyone collected all the stories about the days of Prohibition in St. Pierre, the above would be simply one more in a thousand. Others would relate to more distinguished visitors during the period – the gangster element that had seized control of the liquor distribution system in the U.S. These were the days when the names of "Legs" Diamond, Al Capone, and many another were household words and the stuff of news on every front page in America. In the States, this was crime news, but in St. Pierre the business was completely legal and above board. While the small operators in the U.S. were squeezed out by mobsters, and times were bad for any who attempted to oppose them, in St. Pierre the trade was carried on in respectable office establishments and warehouses.

One of the biggest names in the mob was that of Al Capone, only one on the mainland whose curiosity was piqued by the very existence of St. Pierre, that had been put on the map by the veteran rumrunner Bill McCoy. Word flashed around town one day that Capone had arrived and had checked in at the Hotel Robert. He was accompanied by three bodyguards, the famed and feared Torio brothers who originated in Sicily.

Capone had contacted a St. Pierre merchant and requested a visit to one of the liquor warehouses. With his bodyguards and guide, Capone was given a tour. As the party passed a building with bars on its windows, Capone inquired if this was the local jail. When informed that this was the Treasury Building (a branch of the Bank of France) where all of the island's central funds were safeguarded, the gangster jokingly remarked to his guide, "Well, get in there and clean her out."

The merchant quickly shot back, "Don't do that! I have all my money in there."

This bit of lighthearted repartee spread like wildfire through the community, and hasty measures were immediately taken to organize communication between the Treasury and the police station, just in case Capone meant what he said.

One night during Capone's visit, he and his party decided late in the evening to visit the Café Francais for a drink. The bar was closed, but after a shout by one of the Torio brothers, "Angelina, open up, Al Capone is here," two doors quickly unlocked to admit the fearsome visitor.

The following day, as the visitors toured the waterfront, they stopped by a rumrunner tied up at dockside. A St. Pierre captain was in command of the *Chappel Point*. While talking to the skipper, one of the party offered him a cigar, a gift declined with thanks by the non-smoker. One of the Torio brothers took umbrage at the rebuff and pulled his pistol. Though known locally as a tough seaman, the captain was visibly shaken as he smoked the cigar.

Continuing their stroll through town, the Chicago mobsters took in the shops, the distillers' offices, and all the business establishments, most of which were connected with the liquor trade in one form or another. At one of the larger stores on the waterfront, the employees scurried in fear to call the manager. What does one say to a gangster without fear that a chance remark might be taken the wrong way? The storekeeper found the answer, complimenting Capone on the straw hat he was wearing. The kingpin of the underworld was pleased. "Have it – a souvenir from Al Capone," he replied, handing the man his hat.

Al Capone's hat on display at the Hotel Robert in St. Pierre.
(Photo courtesy of Mr. Lucien Girardin-Dagort)

The skimmer remains on the island to this day, a prized item in the Hotel Robert collection of memorabilia of the days of Prohibition and the visit of Al Capone.

During his visit, Capone also checked up on the problem of the wooden boxes that created noise while being transhipped, resulting in some vessels being arrested by the U.S. Coast Guard.

The *Chappel Point* was a regular visitor to Demerara in British Guyana for a load of rum. (Photo courtesy of Mr. Ted Hennegar)

A solution was found. The liquor would be prepacked into jute sacks, each bottle with a straw cover and ears sewn on the bags so they could easily be transhipped. As this proved popular, the goods would henceforth be pre-bagged at the distillery and only the wooden case would have to be removed in St. Pierre.

This meant that hundreds of thousands of cases became available free of charge to island residents to use for firewood. Boxes were also neatly dismantled and most of the houses built in St. Pierre during the 1920s and early 1930s were built of empty whisky cases.

Today, seventy-five years after repeal, there is still one summer house in St. Pierre that is built of empty whisky cases. It is appropriately named "Cutty Sark Villa," as it is built of empty Scotch whisky of that brand.

* * *

The first half of the 1920s were the halcyon days of the liquor business in St. Pierre.

Operating procedures had been developed by Canadian distillers to get their products into the hands of the smuggling trade without running afoul of their country's laws. The European suppliers had no such problems, and in St. Pierre there were willing and competent distributors for vast amounts of all kinds of alcoholic beverages. Enforcement of the laws of both Canada and the United States was lax, and profits were so great that payoffs were easily afforded.

As the trade grew and fell into the hands of the gangster elements in the U.S., Americans and Canadians alike began a process of tightening up regulations and cleaning house. In 1927, Conservative R. B. Bennett succeeded Arthur Meighen as leader of the Official Opposition. Bennett was strongly critical of Prime Minister Mackenzie King and his Liberal government for its failure to enforce laws that reined in the liquor trade.

As well as hotly pursuing rumrunners and bootleggers off and on its own shores, the American Government pressured the Mackenzie King government to place a total embargo on liquor clearances from Canadian ports to countries under prohibition. The Canadian politicians were in a dilemma. The Great Depression was steadily worsening, and the distilling industry was one of the few flourishing segments of the economy. Both jobs and the revenues generated through the excise taxes were important to the country. The total take from excise tax on liquor is said to have exceeded all collections from personal income taxes in a single year. Adding to the government's problems was the increasing pressure of the Conservative Opposition that favoured co-operation with American policies.

A visiting American buyer with the staff of a St. Pierre liquor warehouse.
(Photo courtesy of E. Derrible)

Bowing to these pressures, the Canadian Government introduced a bill in the House of Commons on March 4, 1930, amending the Canada Export Act, the amended law taking effect on July 1. The result was of considerable benefit to St. Pierre. Because of the new regulations, Canadian distilleries would have to use their "foreign" bases in St. Pierre on an unprecedented scale.

In the general election of 1930, R. B. Bennett defeated Mackenzie King and became Prime Minister. One of his earliest moves was to launch an investigation of the liquor smuggling trade, including the involvement of St. Pierre and Miquelon. Everything was legal and above board on the islands, of course, but investigators were easily able to determine that sizeable amounts of liquor distilled in Canada and exported to St. Pierre were finding their way back home, and evading customs and excise collectors to boot. Even more disturbing were revelations that fortunes were being made in the trade with St. Pierre by Canadian distilleries' sales organizations there and the profits were being laundered through complex financial dealings involving the Canadian Bank of Commerce branch on the island.

As the 1920s waned and the Depression years of the 1930s saw economic hardship assume worldwide proportions, the economy of St. Pierre boomed. In retrospect, while North America and Newfoundland (then an independent Dominion, though going broke financially) floundered in Depression, St. Pierre and Miquelon were enjoying prosperity on a scale never dreamed of. Large, ultra-modern warehouses were being built to store the ever-increasing liquor cargoes arriving almost daily. Nova Scotia shipyards were busy building high-powered rumrunners. There was work for the St. Pierrais, and for many Newfoundlanders. Times had never been better.

As a result of these boom times in St. Pierre, a large number of young ladies from the Burin Peninsula came over to the island and were employed in housework for many families. They learned from their employers the art of French cooking, many married local young men, and some of the best French chefs of the island who ran businesses in the 1950s and 1960s were former Newfoundlanders. Due to Prohibition, the blood had been changed forever. There are very few St. Pierre residents who as a result do not have Newfoundland relatives.

Whisky cases were neatly dismantled and would be used for firewood or to build houses. (Photo courtesy of Mr. Lucien Girardin-Dagort)

Cutty Sark Villa in St. Pierre was built with empty Scotch cases during Prohibition. (Photo courtesy of Mr. Lucien Girardin-Dagort)

Inside walls of Cutty Sark Villa on St. Pierre.
(Photo courtesy of Mr. Lucien Girardin-Dagort)

An old house shingled with liquor crates from the Prohibition era.
(Photo courtesy of Mr. Lucien Girardin-Dagort)

Hotel Robert in St. Pierre, where Al Capone and many others involved in the rumrunning trade stayed while on St. Pierre. (Author collection)

Mini museum of the Prohibition era at the Hotel Robert in St. Pierre.
(Author collection)

Mount Carmel cemetery outside of Chicago where Al Capone is buried.
(Author collection)

Al Capone's grave at the Mount Carmel cemetery outside of Chicago.
(Author collection)

A small village at the tip of the Burin Peninsula.
(Author collection)

A Burin Peninsula village across from St. Pierre.
(Author collection)

RUMRUNNERS VERSUS THE LAW

Clearing from St. Pierre Harbour with a cargo of liquor was the easiest part of the rumrunner's business. Getting rid of the cargo safely posed many more problems and, as detection and pursuit procedures gained in sophistication over the years, the risks involved increased sharply.

Most of the vessels headed for Rum Row outside the twelve-mile limit along the American East Coast, though some rumrunners headed for deliveries to Canadian customers.

The products varied according to destination. Americans were mainly interested in bourbon, Scotch, and rye whiskies, delivered over the side in cases or burlap bags. Canadian customers placed a premium on good dark Demerara rum, sold from the boat in small puncheons, and the nearly pure, white alcohol that was delivered in two-and-a-half-gallon tins or barrels.

In most cases, the rumrunners remained outside territorial limits as soon as they cleared St. Pierre. For the U.S. trade, that generally meant twelve miles or more; in Canada it was twelve miles for Canadian vessels and three for those of British registry, an advantage for Newfoundland ships.

To best tell the story of how the clandestine operations were carried out, here are examples of what happened to some of the ships and their cargoes.

* * *

The *Fanny Powell* loaded a full shipment of whisky in St. Pierre, to be delivered to Joseph's Inlet, near New York. The *Powell* sailed to a position on instructions sent to her captain by a coded message. The identification in this instance had not been the frequently used dollar bill or playing card cut into halves, but a Freemason's ring that the shore party had to produce before taking delivery of the goods.

Just as the final load had been slung over the side, a large four-stack cutter fired warning shots, and the rumrunner's captain was questioned. Asked to explain his presence, the vessel's captain-owner explained that his ship was leaking; he was merely transferring his cargo to another vessel in an effort to save both ship and cargo. The Coast Guard allowed the *Powell* to proceed, but took the shore vessel in tow and impounded ship and cargo. The liquor was transferred to a warehouse on the New York waterfront where seized cargoes were held.

The liquor's owner knew he had lost a battle, but not the war. Following suggestions by his American clients, he engaged New York lawyer Louis Halle, renowned for his successful defences of rumrunners. The case was fought on the grounds that the *Powell* had been in a sinking condition and the judge ruled that the cargo should be released. The *Powell's* owner sailed into New York to pick up his liquor, but when he arrived at the warehouse he discovered that through careless handling and stacking it was impossible to separate his goods from other seized material. A few well-placed, medium-sized bills in the hands of the warehousemen allowed him to remove to his boat quantities of higher-quality liquors than had been seized from his vessel. Clearing New York in a hurry, he hastened to the coast of Maine, where the bottled goods were disposed of without difficulty.

Another rumrunner was the converted Newfoundland steamer the *Zelda*, fitted out to transport 6,000 cases. She made six successful trips, sailing by night to dockside in New Jersey where waiting trucks off-loaded her whisky cargo into the hands of the customers

The seventh such voyage led to her downfall. Intercepted by the Coast Guard, the *Zelda's* master was asked for his manifests, indicating destination and the cargo he was carrying. When satisfactory

Rumrunning vessels had several nameplates on board – they would leave St. Pierre with one name and arrive on Rum Row with another. (Photo courtesy of Mrs. Marie Enguehard)

papers could not be produced, and since the ship was within the twelve-mile limit, the *Zelda* and her crew were placed under arrest and escorted into New York. The seventeen crewmen were lodged in jail, to be released later when bonds were posted by the owners. During their period in the city awaiting trial, the authorities questioned the sailors frequently, seeking information on their involvement with the liquor traffic, but to no avail. Fifty-two days after their arrest, judgment was handed down; the crew was allowed to return home, but the ship and cargo were forfeited.

Perhaps the most famous rumrunning schooner was the *I'm Alone*, owned by Captain Iversen of Lunenburg. The vessel was notable in 1926, in that a radio transmitter had been installed, and an operator hired. He served two years during the period the *I'm Alone* was commanded by Captain H. Heisler, known as "Gow," and Captain Olson. The schooner was powered by two 1,000-horsepower Fairbanks Morse engines. She was the first rumrunning schooner equipped with, then illegal, "ham" radio transmitters that kept in touch with shore-based sets on the U.S. Coast. Orders detailing drop-off points, the known positions of Coast Guard vessels, and other dangers to the trade were communicated by code, changed frequently to foil efforts to decipher it. Code books used on most vessels had lead covers for quick jettisoning, should the ship be searched.

The *I'm Alone*, with a capacity of 6,000 cases of liquor, operated regularly between St. Pierre and the area off Boston. A support vessel, the *No. 174*, worked out of Nova Scotia during summertime and acted as a tender between the *I'm Alone* and Marblehead, Massachusetts. The *No. 174* was powered by four aircraft engines and had an effective speed of thirty-five knots. Consumption of gasoline was about seventy-five gallons an hour; the smaller boat would refuel from gasoline drums on the deck of the *I'm Alone*.

The *No. 174*'s superior speed always enabled her to outrun the Coast Guard, but there was at least one narrow escape. Being chased by a cutter, a shower of bullets fell on the *No. 174*, one of them striking the captain and igniting a box of matches in a trouser pocket.

The support vessel was available only during the summer season. During the remainder of the year, the *I'm Alone* depended on shore-based boats to ferry liquor to land. On one winter trip, the schooner was forced to remain for a lengthy period off the Massachusetts coast. She was having engine problems, and fuel was running low. Unable to enter an American port for repairs, her

The schooner *I'm Alone*, an early rumrunning vessel, was gunned down and sunk by the U.S. Coast Guard in international waters when she refused to stop.
(Photo courtesy of the Maritime Museum of the Atlantic, Halifax)

skipper was forced to jettison 1,000 cases of liquor and return home. The owner, discouraged with this loss, brought the schooner back to Yarmouth and sold her.

The *I'm Alone*'s radio operator returned to St. Pierre. On his arrival, he was introduced by a liquor trader to two brothers known as Louis and Maxi, prominent in the New York liquor trade. Louis had two large vessels, the *Standard Coaster* and *Harbor Trader*, able to carry 7,000 cases. These were the names used while off the American Coast; in St. Pierre they changed identities and became the *Owl* and *Rex*. They resembled large ocean-going tugs and operated regularly between St. Pierre and Newark, New Jersey. Their season was from September until May, that period of the year with longer nights, to aid their clandestine voyages and unloading. They sailed boldly up the river to Newark, without lights but with a local pilot who was in the pay of the owners. All the way upriver, bridges would be raised and trains would stop to allow the dark vessels to pass, everyone paid off for their silence.

The *Standard Coaster (Owl)* was not equipped with radio, so her owner signed on the *I'm Alone*'s operator and installed transmitting equipment. The results were so satisfactory that in due course her sister vessel was similarly equipped. Numbers were used as codes by the rumrunners. With the way cleared through onshore contacts, the vessels would sail to Newark where approximately 100 men would be ready on the dock for a quick unloading into trucks; the crew could handle 1,000 cases an hour in a race against the clock and the coming daylight. There were times when the two ships would have to sail prematurely to make the twelve-mile limit before daybreak, without having completely discharged their cargoes.

"Louis" kept in continuous contact with the ships by code, and if problems arose he could order an immediate change of course. Sometimes it was possible to complete two trips in a month, depending upon the moon. On the way south the ships stopped in Liverpool, Nova Scotia, for coal and provisions, and to await a favourable quarter of the moon. Louis travelled from New York to meet the ships and to pay the crews' wages. In those times a radio operator earned $250 a month, with a bonus of about that same amount for every successful trip.

In the depths of winter, they also made deliveries up the Delaware River to Philadelphia. Again, a well-paid pilot would be employed to navigate without lights to the discharge point in Philadelphia, at the coal docks. On one occasion, with time for escape running out, the rumrunners were tied up to nearby coal barges and camouflaged while their crews spent the day in a hotel. With the arrival of darkness, the return voyage downriver was accomplished without anyone on shore having noticed.

In December of 1928, the *Harbor Trader (Rex)*, after several successful trips, was upriver and had managed to off-load 6,000 of her 7,000 cases. The owner decided that time was becoming short for a getaway and she should sail immediately, despite having part of her cargo still aboard. After casting off, the captain made what could be classified as a navigational error by sailing too close to an illuminated buoy. A cutter standing nearby, with all lights doused, spotted the ship's silhouette and gave chase, apprehending the rumrunner. A boarding party soon ordered the crew to the stern of the vessel and took the *Rex* in tow to Staten Island. Later she moved to the barge office dock in New York Harbour and was placed under guard.

Louis Halle, a New York lawyer, represented the owner and crew in court in Brooklyn, and they were soon free on bail. After being there for around three weeks, the men were released but the *Rex* was impounded with the balance of her cargo.

However, the rumrunning trade was so profitable that replacements were soon on the way. Two new vessels, termed "banana boats" from their shape, were under construction in Liverpool, Nova Scotia, in the Gardner Shipyards. To some observers, the banana boats resembled submarines, as they sat very low in the water when fully laden. One of the new boats could carry the equivalent of 2,500 cases packed in burlap bags; the other was equipped with tanks, as a small tanker. A cargo of Scotch malt whisky, arriving from Scotland in barrels, was transferred by means of huge funnels to the tanks, all connected with the move of whisky marvelling at the aroma released as it enveloped the workers.

Discharge of the cargo was even more ingenious than the loading of the vessel. Close by Sea Girt Beach, New Jersey, stood a mock-up of a gas station. From the vessel a few yards off shore, a flexible hose led to the service station's underground tanks and the cargo was safely transferred, a ruse that continued successfully until the end of Prohibition.

The story of the *I'm Alone* wasn't over, as she was sold to new interests and continued her career in the rumrunning trade for a short while.

Across the border, President Calvin Coolidge signed on March 2, 1929, what became known as the Jones Law, providing stiff new penalties for violation of the Volstead Act. Five years imprisonment and fines of up to $10,000 were provided to give teeth to the new law, and the effect became immediately apparent. Five days after passing of the Jones Law, two U.S. Coast Guard cutters closed in on a Lunenburg rumrunning schooner after a long pursuit. The *I'm Alone* was 200 miles beyond U.S. territorial limits with a cargo of liquor loaded in British Honduras, as well as 1,500 cases from St. Pierre. Her captain, John Thomas Randell, had encountered difficulty in disposing of the St. Pierre cargo, and when the Coast Guard cutter issued several warnings to heave to during the chase, he refused to stop, confident that his distance at sea would protect his ship. It was not to be; the pursuer opened fire and USCG *Dexter* pumped enough of her four-pounder shells into the *I'm Alone* to sink her. The upshot was a celebrated three-nation international incident. One man, a French citizen, died after exposure in the water, while Randell and his crew were taken to jail in New Orleans. The legal aftermath remained hot for years, not settled until 1935, when Canada's Chief Justice and a U.S. Supreme Court Justice awarded $50,666 to Canada, plus an official apology from the United States, while Randell and his crew were awarded $25,666 and were exonerated. The owners of the ship and the liquor received nothing.

Mr. Revert and another crew member on deck of the *Arethusa*.
(Photo courtesy of Mrs. Revert collection)

Gertrude Light, one of the very few women who went to Rum Row, with the cook of the *Arethusa*, Mr. Revert. (Photo courtesy of Mrs. Revert collection)

Mr. Revert, cook of the *Arethusa*, on deck of the vessel.
(Photo courtesy of Mrs. Revert collection)

As the Coast Guard was getting better organized, rumrunners purchased surplus sub chasers from WWI to carry their prized cargoes at much higher speed.
(Photo courtesy of the Maritime Museum of the Atlantic, Halifax, McBride collection)

Modern rumrunners copied from sub chasers were being built at Nova Scotia shipyards for the American syndicates.
(Photo courtesy of the Maritime Museum of the Atlantic, Halifax, McBride collection)

Secret code used by a rumrunning vessel to communicate with a contact on shore. (Document courtesy of Mr. Henri Moraze)

Two rumrunning vessels transferring cargo at sea.
(Photo courtesy of Captain R. C. Butt)

A barrel of rum going over the side to a high-speed launch to carry it ashore.
(Photo courtesy of Dr. G. Robinson)

Marvita – known as a banana boat. This vessel was a tanker that would carry bulk whisky and hose it ashore. The *Marvita* was purchased after Prohibition by the Newfoundland customs service and was used as a patrol vessel to chase rumrunners. (Photo courtesy of the Maritime Museum of the Atlantic, Halifax, McBride collection)

THE COAST GUARD'S WAR ON RUMRUNNERS

Despite all their imaginative methods for evading detection in landing goods that were illegal in the countries of their destination, rumrunners inevitably were bound to cross the paths of the United States Coast Guard.

The situations differed on American and Canadian shores. As the illicit trade grew to mammoth proportions, the U.S. Coast Guard refined its methods and acquired constantly new and more powerful ships in an attempt to match wits and equipment with the rumrunners. In the end, enforcement of the National Prohibition Act nearly amounted to a state of warfare with the USCG vessels heavily armed and quick on the trigger. Bodily harm and death was always near at hand in encounters between the two sides.

The patrolling Coast Guard ships, equipped with powerful searchlights and machine guns, made life exciting for those seeking to evade them. When a rumrunner was caught, the cargo of liquor would be confiscated, generally the minimum penalty the owner could expect. It was an axiom that the Coast Guard vessels were themselves well-stocked with liquor; their crews were experienced sailor men well-acquainted with alcohol in all its varieties from their days in the merchant marine in all parts of the world. Sometimes it was said that a Coast Guard's zeal in intercepting a rumrunner was in direct proportion to the boat's current stock in the liquor cabinets aboard.

Besides the classical manoeuvres of standing outside the twelve-mile limit and putting cargoes over the side into fast shore launches, catches were hidden away while standing off shore. Witness the case of the yacht *Swan*, specially designed for the trade. The rum-runner *Isabel H* would load in St. Pierre and keep the *Swan* supplied on a scheduled basis. The entire keel of the yacht had a double lining. Access to the storage compartments was through a guest room; a drawer could be pulled out, allowing entry for one man to the double partitions that would accommodate five-gallon barrels of malt whisky.

Another ruse concerned the *Marylyn,* ostensibly a fishing vessel. She had plenty of power with two eighty-horsepower engines, but her builders did much more than install the power plant in a conventional manner. Beneath the engines there was space sufficient for a man to stand and to accommodate comfortably, 1,000 cases of whisky. The Coast Guard was suspicious of the *Marylyn*, as with most other vessels that arrived from waters to the north. On one occasion they intercepted her and she remained tied to a dock while Preventive Service officers combed her from stem to stern, to no avail. There was irony in the search that lasted a month, because the *Marylyn* sat serenely in the water, fully laden with her 1,000 cases of whisky. Probably only pulling her from the water would have revealed the truth, for this most unusual fishing vessel drew sixteen feet of water. As a further ruse, the ship, after connecting with her mother ship at sea, would throw off suspicion by actually fishing for a few days.

Recounted here are only a few of the hoaxes and subterfuges used by dozens of rumrunners to outwit the law enforcement men, both on and off shore. There was adventure and excitement in the business of getting liquor from St. Pierre into the hands of the distributors, though it was the latter who pocketed the huge profits from the trade. In the passage of time, as Coast Guard methods became more sophisticated, many ships' crews were caught and dealt with by the law, but that was part of the game, a risk accepted and well understood. There probably never was a time when the enforcers could truly claim to be fully on top of the situation, and vast quantities of liquor continued to reach customers in the speakeasies of the United States.

Off the Canadian Coast, shootings were a rarity and in most cases accidental. The Preventive Service cutters performed their function with courtesy but firmness. In many cases the hunters and hunted were personally acquainted, sometimes shipmates of former times.

During the early years of Prohibition, the odds were stacked on the side of the rumrunners. The U.S. Coast Guard was poorly supplied with ships to patrol the long coastline from Maine to Florida. They were unable to crack the rumrunners' crude but effective codes, and the equipping of vessels with wireless communication added to the hunted ships' chances of evading pursuers.

However, with experience, plus more and better ships and new tactics, the odds were shortened. Teams were put together to crack coded messages and to thwart the rumrunners' best efforts. The "dirty tricks" squad, in possession of a code, sometimes was successful in luring rumrunners into traps with fake messages and changed orders. On the liquor boats, the radio operator often became the key man, able to judge between "real" orders and those hammered out on the keys of Coast Guard operators.

After loading in St. Pierre, the first hurdle was to travel undetected to points off the American Coast. Then came the problem of contacting shore-based agents who had their own problems in running out beyond the twelve-mile limit to pick up their loads. On many occasions the fast rumrunning boats, lying low in the water, would dash into secluded coves and sheltered bays to get rid of their loads and hurry back beyond the limit before daybreak.

Delivery messages would be picked up by the rumrunners as they hovered forty to sixty miles off shore. The game of chess usually began during the late afternoon or early evening, the rumrunners going to pre-arranged rendezvous just outside the limit. Offloading would begin around midnight and be completed in time for all boats to be clear of the area during the hours of darkness.

One ploy devised by the "dirty tricks" squad of the Coast Guard was to send a note to a rumrunning skipper thanking him for his co-operation with the Preventive Service, perhaps by passing on details of operations being conducted at sea. Sometimes money would be enclosed with the message, and it would be arranged that the gangster syndicate would acquire a copy of such information about ostensible collusion. The result would be elimination of the captain involved, executed by the "mob," often with his body encased in a "concrete overcoat" and disposed at sea.

Though built for the trade and heavily engined, rumrunners' crafts were frail vessels. Speed, stealth, and daring were their crews' only protection against the heavily powered USCG patrol ships, manned by hardened sailors eager for any kind of work in tough economic times when jobs were few. Many of them were other than American citizens.

In 1925, the Canadian protective service of the Customs and Excise department deployed fifteen patrol vessels to cover the whole of the Atlantic Coast and the St. Lawrence River. The Royal Canadian Mounted Police took over this service in 1932.

Tales of the rumrunners and their adversaries became a legend during the era of Prohibition, a segment of history during which St. Pierre and Miquelon were household names on the pages of newspapers and popular literature in a manner never before imagined.

There were no radars in those days. The vessel had to be seen. Imaginative ways had been devised to try and escape the Coast Guard. Rumrunners would sometimes have a red-hot pipe going through their engine room. If the Coast Guard was too close, they would put used lubricating oil on this pipe, which would result in a heavy, black smokescreen which would mask their whereabouts and sometimes enable them to escape.

A high-powered launch equipped with aircraft engines capable of thirty-five knots would be used to transport alcohol from a runner ship to shore.
(Photo courtesy of Knickles Studio, Lunenburg, NS)

A shore boat from Rhode Island awaiting the arrival of a liquor-laden rumrunner.
(Photo courtesy of Mr. James Miller)

Manuel Ferris and companion. He was known in Rhode Island during the Prohibition era as the Rhode Island rum king. (Photo courtesy of Mr. James Miller)

Rumrunner Herb Cavaca and companion. He was another Rhode Island rumrunner. (Photo courtesy of Mr. James Miller)

If the landing boat was sighted by the Coast Guard, the Rhode Island gang would dump their jute sacks into Naraganset Bay. Each bag would have a sponge that had been dipped in fuel oil, leaving a small streak that would allow a diver to go down and retrieve the liquor. (Photo courtesy of Mr. James Miller)

U.S. Coast Guard cutter on patrol off the U.S. Coast. (Author collection)

Some rumrunners went equipped with red-hot pipes going through the engine room. If they were pursued by the Coast Guard they would put used lube oil on the pipes, creating a thick black smoke and try to make their getaway.
(Photo courtesy of Mr. Pierre Gautier)

Seized barrels of rum being carried off to a customs warehouse in Pictou, Nova Scotia. (Photo courtesy of Captain R. C. Butt)

Rumrunning schooner *St. Pierraise* on station to deliver alcohol to the Gulf of St. Lawrence. (Photo courtesy of Mrs. Marie Enguehard)

St. Pierraise **– rumrunning schooner at Hooping Harbour, White Bay, NL, 1933.**
(Photo courtesy of Mrs. Marie Enguehard)

Rumrunning schooner *Dorothy M. Smart* in the Gulf of St. Lawrence.
(Photo courtesy of Captain R.C. Butt)

PIRACY: AN EVER-PRESENT THREAT

The *Mulhouse* was a 1,900-ton freighter owned by the Morue Francaise interests, of France and St. Pierre. She had taken aboard a cargo of 36,404 cases of whiskies, champagnes, liqueurs, and cognacs and sailed from Europe for the American Coast in June 1924.

The steamer, with a crew of twenty-eight, arrived off Fire Island, New York. Standing outside the twelve-mile limit, she waited for several days for a coded message from her owners as to how the cargo should be delivered.

News of the riches in her holds attracted plenty of attention on Rum Row, accustomed to the arrival of much smaller vessels. Those 36,404 cases of fine liquor were exciting and tantalizing to the thirsty throats in the speakeasies of New York. Small boats hovered nearby, ready to make deals, but the *Mulhouse*'s skipper waited for his orders by wireless.

Two or three miles away lay a rumrunning schooner, the *Patara*. On June 13, an officer of the *Patara* boarded the *Mulhouse* to discuss prices and quantities of liquor; he returned on the same mission several times between then and June 24. Other small vessels with would-be purchasers aboard also visited the *Mulhouse*. On June 17, the Coast Guard vessel *Kickapoo* circled the *Mulhouse*, but there was no communication between the ships.

On the morning of June 24, the *Patara* raised anchor and tied up on the port side of the *Mulhouse*. Three men climbed aboard – a bootlegger, his assistant, and his cashier. Two negotiators on the steamer invited the trio into the lounge, where they began inspecting ledgers showing the breakdown of brands, quantities, and prices. The prospective buyer was making notes, when suddenly he laid down his pen and pulled a revolver from his pocket, ordering "hands up." The other two men from the *Patara* also produced pistols, and within moments a further two *Patara* men arrived, also armed. The *Mulhouse* officers were searched for weapons. During this swift seizure, the *Mulhouse* deck crew had been busy securing lines to the *Patara*. Only seven or eight men had been seen on the smaller *Patara*, but more quickly appeared from their hiding place below decks.

On the starboard side of the *Mulhouse*, another small vessel arrived unnoticed and tied up. Crews from the two rumrunners took the steamer's seamen by surprise and quickly overcame resistance, the captain and three crew members held as hostages. There was no wireless alarm sent from the vessel as the radio shack had quickly been seized and the transmitter demolished.

A strange flotilla of small boats now assembled around the *Mulhouse*. First to come alongside for a load was the *Quaco Queen*, the crew of the *Mulhouse* forced at gunpoint to unload their vessel. Such a frenzy of unloading activity then took place that the steamer's crew was not even allowed time for meals.

While this was taking place, the Coast Guard cutter *Manhattan* approached. Her captain shouted to the bridge of the *Mulhouse* to inquire if everything was normal, and the captain, a revolver levelled at him, was forced to wave the cutter away with a hand signal that all was well. It was the last the *Mulhouse* would see of the Coast Guard.

The next rumrunner to be loaded was the schooner *Tessy and Aubrey*. The weather had worsened and the pirates had the *Mulhouse* raise anchor on three occasions in hopes of finding some shelter from the heavy seas, though they could not move far from the Fire Island Lightship. Then came the schooner *Genevieve*, taking aboard as much as they could carry of the *Mulhouse*'s cargo.

Eventually, all except 1,231 cases were removed from the pirate ship. The chief of the looters pointed out that this amount was being left aboard to prevent the *Mulhouse* entering New York Harbour where she would face arrest.

On July 3, the pirates had completed their work. The worn-out crew was locked into the bow section of the ship, and the captain secured in his cabin. A vital engine part was removed and placed in care of two of the *Mulhouse*'s crew who were needed on deck to let go the lines of the getaway launch, the *Navy Away*. The crewmen were warned not to interfere with the launch's departure, on pain of being gunned down. All weapons from the *Mulhouse* had been thrown into the sea.

During their ordeal the *Mulhouse* men took note of the flotilla of small craft that had taken part in the looting of the ship. Among other schooners there had been the *Catherine Mary*, registered in Nassau, Bahamas, the *Clark Corkum*, the *Maud Thornhill*, and others, all seeming to have been freshly painted, as though a touch-up job had been done quickly to conceal their true identities. Names of the craft were known to the *Mulhouse* crew, who believed the pirates had borrowed the names for the occasion.

Aboard the *Mulhouse* the pirates had continually threatened their prisoners, driving them unmercifully with the unloading, and brutalizing them throughout the period. The looters drank heavily in the officers' quarters, sang, and quarrelled. For amusement they taunted the terrified crew, alternately threatening death, or assuming benign poses claiming that they should be looked upon as "The Lord's joyous children." As well as the liquor cargo, they looted the ship's safe, smashed bottles indiscriminately, and tossed overboard valuable portions of the ship's stores and equipment. Winches were wrecked as the pirates used them for playthings. During their stay on board, they transformed the *Mulhouse* into a floating derelict.

Overtones of bloodshed occurred when, on the second day of the piracy, some of the *Mulhouse* crewmen were forced at gunpoint to stow cases of liquor in the *Patara*'s hold. Plainly visible on the pirate ship were patches of blood and empty shell casings, leading to a belief that the *Patara* herself had been hijacked earlier in a bloody gun battle.

The year after this *Mulhouse* piracy, the French schooner *Mary I* lay at anchor in the outer harbour of St. Pierre, fully loaded with 4,000 cases of whisky. She had recently been purchased by French interests, and her new French captain was ashore completing paperwork prior to sailing for the American Coast.

During this time, her former captain, while she had been under British registry, was still aboard and he seized the opportunity to hijack the *Mary I*. Pistol in hand, he ordered the crew to hoist sail. Seven of the crew obeyed, and two who refused were savagely beaten. The cook, with a broken arm, and the second man leaped into a dory to escape, and by the time they were able to reach port on the way to hospital, the *Mary I* was under full sail and almost out of sight.

Officers of the maritime administration of St. Pierre gave chase to the schooner in a small tug, with gendarmes armed with rifles aboard. The *Mary I* showed her heels and soon was out of sight. Some vessels were equipped with wireless, and a general alarm was broadcast to all shipping in the area that might intercept a message to be on the lookout for the fugitive schooner. One trawler, the *Asie*, heard the appeal as it sailed close by the *Mary I*; she altered course and took up the chase, which proved to be a long one as the fleeing schooner under full sail had as good a speed as the steam-powered trawler. The *Asie*'s chief had a major problem; he was running low on fuel. In fact, the vessel had been making for St. Pierre to replenish coal, water, and provisions when she was diverted.

Between seven and eight o'clock, the wind did decrease, slowing down the schooner and allowing the *Asie* to come within 200 feet of the fugitive, but just as the captain of the trawler hailed the vessel and ordered her to stop, new gusts of wind allowed the schooner to increase its speed. Despite the trawler's 10.5 knots, the *Mary I* again pulled ahead.

The chase continued, and for a while the steam vessel had the advantage, though by now it was almost out of coal. In a last-ditch effort, the trawler captain closed on the *Mary I* and rammed her, damaging the mainsail. A further order to stop was accompanied by a threat to ram the sailing ship amidships. In short order, a dory pulled away from the fugitive schooner, three men rowing toward the trawler. The other four crewmen refused to surrender, but as the infuriated captain again headed his trawler straight toward the schooner and issued a five-minute ultimatum, the seamen gave themselves up and soon were locked in the fish hold with their mates.

With the schooner in tow, the captain of the trawler approached St. Pierre, to be greeted by a flotilla of dories and a hero's welcome. Feelings against the hijacking crew were running high along the waterfront. Had the police not intervened and carted the eight sailors off to jail in a covered truck, there might have been rough mob justice meted out.

These are but two of a host stories of adventure in the days of smuggling and rumrunning on the Atlantic Coast. Tales of seizure and hijack, of crime and rough justice, of fortunes made and men and ships lost characterized the days of the rumrunning trade. The risks were great but the stakes were high. It was a desperate game.

The French trawler *Asie* caught up with the hijacked *Mary I* – which was
fully laden with a load of liquor – seen in St. Pierre Harbour.
(Photo courtesy of Briand-Ozon collection)

A rumrunner on Rum Row off Fire Island, New York.
(Photo courtesy of Captain R. C. Butt)

MURDER AND ITS AFTERMATH

A whole new way of life came to St. Pierre during the era of Prohibition. Gone were the days when men sailed in schooners for the Banks or pushed off the beach in dories for the inshore fishery. There were plenty of jobs on shore, and the colony finances had never before known such prosperity.

In 1924, for instance, the gross income, mostly from the small per-case levy on liquor, netted the government 10,910,000 francs, nearly three times its expenditures, which in that year used up only 3,300,000 francs. There were accumulated reserves on hand of 22,010,000 francs.

The windfall profits from liquor taxes enabled the government to undertake numerous public works projects. Given priority were improvements to the harbour installations for the benefit of fishing vessels that regularly made St. Pierre their base, and to enhance facilities for the ships of the liquor trade. Dredging, new wharves, and better breakwaters were undertaken in the interests of shipping.

In the town there was overall an air of prosperity. In 1922, the total commercial activity of the island was calculated at 96,000,000 francs. A year later, prosperity without precedent skyrocketed this activity to an astounding 298,000,000 francs.

However, it was well recognized that there was a price to be paid for such relative affluence. No one was blind to the fact that the profits came from smuggling and bootlegging in the United States, plus a measure from the Canadian trade.

The business was concentrated in the hands of the underworld and the so-called Syndicate. On occasion, leaders of the mob visited St. Pierre to view first-hand the source of the liquid wealth they were handling.

The night of February 18, 1924, was one to be remembered in St. Pierre. A local liquor merchant organized a gala ball in honour of visiting customers from the States. Sixty guests were invited for the occasion. At midnight a procession around the ballroom saw each guest carrying a bottle of champagne. Leading the grand march, and crowned with a paper headdress, was an American visitor who was installed as "King of American Prohibition." Later in the evening there was a ceremonial bathing of the feet in champagne.

A tally of the party's consumption has remained: 144 bottles of champagne, four bottles of Malaga wine, four of port, three bottles of Black & White Scotch, and thirty-seven bottles of beer. The celebration that lasted most of the night, including musicians and food, cost a mere $300. No wonder St. Pierre earned a reputation for being able to provide the best for a pittance.

Most times the visiting Americans would be accompanied by their lady friends. Rather than exerting a civilizing effect, the presence of the fair sex provoked lovers' quarrels and violence. On one memorable occasion, only prompt action prevented one jilted lady from committing suicide by jumping into the harbour.

Managers for the Canadian distilleries that were using St. Pierre as a transhipment base tried to maintain a good corporate image in St. Pierre. In a courtesy visit to the Catholic bishop, a trio involved heavily in the liquor trade listened with interest as the prelate mentioned his financial problems in the completion of a new school. It was no coincidence that the following morning a messenger delivered to the bishop a cheque for $10,000, sufficient to finish the building project. The bishop suitably acknowledged the donation, in English, during his sermon the following Sunday morning.

Throughout the period of Prohibition, the harbour was crowded with vessels from many nations, bringing goods to St. Pierre, as well as loading for Rum Row. The bars remained open until five or six o'clock in the morning, and the champagne flowed all night. The heavy drinking inevitably led to violence and sometimes the settling of scores. One night, a rumrunner, Nicholas Bazilis Makris, entered a bar and headed straight for Gustave Karlsen, the engineer of a Norwegian vessel that was in port unloading a liquor cargo. Most rumrunners were armed, and Makris walked straight up to Karlsen and shot him point-blank in the chest. Another Norwegian, Knute Henderson, attempted to intervene and was himself wounded by a second shot from Makris's pistol.

Makris, also known in rumrunning circles as Nick Carros, fled from the bar and sought refuge on the *Cote Nord*. It seems almost unbelievable that on an island as small as St. Pierre a murderer could escape detection, but such proved to be the case. While Karlsen lay dying in hospital, Makris was being hidden by his friends. Police searched the *Cote Nord* while she lay at anchor for the next two days, but he was not discovered. After the whole island had been combed, ships were authorized to clear the port, and permission was extended to the *Cote Nord*. Much later it was learned that Makris's shipmates had foiled the search party by rolling the fugitive in one of the vessel's sails and hoisting him partway up the mast to thwart the police.

Though the murderer had escaped, criminal proceedings were carried out in the St. Pierre courtroom. Makris, twenty-six, was convicted *in absentia* on March 18, 1929, and sentenced to life imprisonment at hard labour for his murder of Karlsen.

The penalty for murder in France was death by guillotine, but in St. Pierre the people had, by an unwritten consent, decided that one such experience was sufficient. The last execution had taken place in the late 1800s and the grisly event was still fresh in the minds of the islanders. Joseph Neel, a fisherman, had knifed to death a fellow fisherman from Dog Island during a drunken brawl. The prosecutor demanded the death penalty as a deterrent, as there had been similar crimes in the past.

Neel was found guilty and sentenced to death. There was no guillotine on the island, and one had to be brought from the French Caribbean island colony of Martinique.

Several months passed before the day of execution arrived. Neel was transported during the early hours of morning, in a horse-drawn covered wagon, to the public square where the guillotine had been erected. A large crowd assembled to witness the execution.

It had been difficult to find an executioner, but finally a habitual drunkard serving a jail sentence agreed to play the role in return for release from his cell and the payment of a sum of money.

The prisoner was bound and placed under the guillotine, face down where he could see his coffin, the bottom lined with sawdust. At the last minute the executioner panicked and refused to perform his grim task. The condemned man struggled and screamed and strained against his bonds.

Finally, the executioner agreed to do his job, and after several long minutes he tripped the big blade. However, much worse was yet to come; Neel's frantic struggle had perhaps twisted the frame of the guillotine, preventing the smooth descent of the blade. Whatever the cause, the heavy blade only partially completed its grisly task. The job had to be finished with a butcher knife.

Is it any wonder the memories of that bloody sight, North America's only guillotine execution, weighed heavily upon the people of St. Pierre, to the extent that by common consent there would never be another? It was for this reason that the death sentence was not imposed on Nicholas Bazilis Makris, even in his absence, in the little courtroom that day in March 1929.

The bar where the murder had taken place was the Café Francais. The bullet that had killed the Norwegian ended up lodged deeply in the wooden floor and remained there.

In the late 1960s, the Café Francais was sold and torn down to make way for new construction. One local resident took some of the wood from the structure to use for firewood. Some of the wood remained in his basement for years and years. In 1995, when he was cutting some of the hardwood flooring, the bullet fell out. It was retrieved and is now on display along with other Prohibition items at the Hotel Robert.

Cote Nord – typical early rumrunning schooner. This is the vessel on which
Makris was hidden in the sail after the murder of a Norwegian engineer.
(Author collection)

**Rumrunner *Isabel H* with rubber fenders alongside waiting at Rum Row to
transfer a liquor shipment to a smaller shore base transfer vessel.**
(Photo courtesy of Dr. G. Robinson)

HANDWRITING ON THE WALL

In 1932, there was an election in the U.S. One candidate had made an appeal to the American populace, stating that Prohibition had accomplished nothing for the Americans, that people were drinking more than ever before, and that as a result, it had created a strong Mafia. He told them that if he was elected he would repeal Prohibition.

He was elected in November 1932 and immediately started to work on his election promises.

On February 16, 1933, the U.S. Senate voted in a majority of sixty-three to thirty-five to submit a measure for repeal of the Eighteenth Amendment. Four days later, the House of Representatives concurred with the Senate resolution by 289 to 121.

As a result of the election and the votes of the Senate and Congress, the cozy arrangements for the receiving, storage, and shipping of liquor products from St. Pierre, with orders being issued from Montreal, and the goods forwarded by rumrunners for delivery in the U.S., began to fall apart in 1933.

By late February, "the organization" was still very much in effect. There was so much stock on hand in New York, shipments from St. Pierre were suspended during that month, and the outlook for March was far from rosy. On the island there was one lot of 1,800 cases of rye whisky manufactured by the defunct Lindsay Distillery, and owned by "The Old Pool," so a liquidator had been appointed in Montreal to clear the goods. An offer to purchase was made by an independent St. Pierre merchant, through his Montreal broker, who was dealing with the liquidator. However, the broker advised the St. Pierre man that "Bronfmans" would not let it go at that price; naturally they want to protect the "organization."

Because of the so-called "organization," also known as the "pool," in the early part of 1933, independent dealers were unable to purchase any rye whisky from the distillers' warehouses in St. Pierre, as this might upset the market.

Managers of the distillers' St. Pierre outlets convened at their Montreal offices in early January, to discuss prices, among other matters. From this meeting came the word to expect increases in price for rye and bourbon by $6.00 a case. By April the situation was little changed, though there were rumours in St. Pierre that "some of the boys were not satisfied" with the situation.

Two months later, the U.S. Government did away with restrictions on doctors' prescriptions for liquor to be used for medicinal purposes. Now that physicians could issue as many prescriptions as they pleased, drugstores braced themselves for a rush of business. The prescriptions covered rye and bourbon only, and rumours circulating at the time had it that druggists would be selling pints for $1.50. The usual doctor's prescription cost $1.00, and with a projected price of $2.50 a pint, the bootleggers faced new problems. Canadian distillers, as well, worried that their rye and bourbon business might be coming to an end.

In May, the situation worsened, if anything. Schooners returning from Demerara were clearing their rum cargoes at bargain prices; rum on the coast was going overboard for as low as $1.75 a gallon.

Political events seriously affected the trade of St. Pierre. Stocks owned by Canadian distillers were being held in anticipation of a flood of orders from the U.S., and no new stocks were arriving. It was a commonly held view that there probably would be a shortage by the end of the year and that prices would go sky-high. By the end of June, speculations in shares of liquor stocks excited the stock market. Walker's common stock rose from $5.00 to $35.00,

Consolidated Distilleries from $0.50 to $9.00, Distillers Corporation from $5.00 to $20.00. The public fully expected that the distillers were poised for huge amounts of new business in the U.S. following repeal, now regarded as certain to pass.

On August 1, a rumour circulated in Montreal that Consolidated Distilleries had sold a parcel of 38,000 cases to a U.S. distillery, though a week later this was denied on the basis that some Consolidated directors did not want to sell at the rumoured price. Through gossip and reports emanated from many sources, the liquor trade was in a state of gleeful anticipation. In the first week of August, Distillers Corporation, B.C. Distillery, United Distilleries, and Consolidated Distilleries raised their prices on rye and bourbon to $9.00 for quarts; forty ounces of Scotch were going for $12.50 per case.

In this connection, as an insight into the type of communication that took place during those latter days of the liquor trade, here's the reply a St. Pierre merchant received from Montreal, dated August 19, to an earlier query on what was doing in the business.

"Received your letter and note the 20 Tokay was delivered. Many Thanks.

Lots of things are happening here. Bronfman, B.C., U.D., and Consolidated have made a price agreement, quarts $9.00, pints $10.00. Any customer who owes money must pay before he can buy from anyone.

Walker – not in above agreement. Prices Cdn Club $6.50 and $7.00; this morning they raised them to $10.00 and $11.00. They sold all their goods except Canadian Club at St. Pierre and Bermuda (43,000 cases – $28,000). They are now selling only Canadian Club. 43,000 cases were sold to an operator, then turned over to a U.S. distillery syndicate to be shipped to the U.S. after repeal. I was working on this deal but got double-crossed.

Distillers here are swamped with inquiries from

U.S. distillers. But they do not want to sell just now. This will certainly be a lot of business at St. P. and a shortage of goods. The 38,000 case deal will probably go through like I told you.

There will be no more bargains. We missed a good bet with the Lindsay goods . . .

There was a lot of goods (rye, bourbon) shipped from St. Pierre lately. This was on account of the expected price rise.

The reason for prices going up is that the U.S. legitimate enquiries are making the distilleries independent and they are not anxious to sell to the operators except at high prices.

Old Orkney: Am working on this. There is some hitch regarding the label requirements for the U.S. market. These goods (blended goods) apparently have to contain a lot of information reblend – pure food laws etc. Could you give me an age certificate on this merchandise, also a certificate of origin? Please advise how many H&S you have.

Also advise any stocks of rye you have, bulk or case goods. Give strength, age, origin etc. See if there are any parcels of rye or bourbon for there (Folquet, Chartier, etc.)

But do not mention anything of above as we might be able to do ourselves some good.

Wish I had a big backer, could have made a lot of money buying merchandise.

Am trying to sell all my rum to a U.S. distillery at $3.00 a gallon in puncheons.

Re Piper – Heard there was a demand for this parcel, but at 240 francs it's too high for us. Why don't you wire them and ask for a cut price for the whole lot? Then you could let me know. If I sold it, well and good, if not we lose nothing.

Could you find out without raising any suspi-
cions what you want it for? . . .
Everybody is in the liquor business in N.Y. and
they don't know very much about it. There's going to
be lots of money lost . . .
Your friend – Rod."

In the third week of September, Consolidated Distilleries had completed the sale of its 38,000 cases, and prices being quoted by Distillers Corporation and Consolidated Distilleries were $13.00 per case for quarts. The "organization" had been successful in its policy of sticking together on prices, as the latter had about doubled from what they had been earlier in the year.

At the end of September, 40,000 cases of champagne were on their way to St. Pierre, but the arrival of French wines was given a cool reception. European shippers were eager to continue to do business, especially to keep their brand names before the U.S. public, until repeal should become a fact. On the other hand, the Canadian distillers wanted to push their own products after repeal and were not interested in furthering the reputations of champagne, cognac, and Scotch whisky makers, especially as it was recognized that the Canadians would lose their markets for European goods after repeal when former U.S. agents resumed business directly.

The year 1933 saw great changes in St. Pierre. The handwriting was on the wall for the lucrative smuggling business, and repeal of the Eighteenth Amendment would once again see St. Pierre revert to its time-honoured role as a small fishing station. It looked as though the end of good times could not be far away.

Mr. James Miller was a watcher on the small Rhode Island shore boats that would await the arrival of the liquor-laden rumrunner.
(Photo courtesy of Mr. James Miller)

THE COMING OF REPEAL

Although the last months of 1933 signalled to almost everyone the imminent end of Prohibition, activity in rumrunning from St. Pierre continued at a brisk pace.

Julien Moraze received a letter from a Massachusetts man that described the typical clandestine nature of the business. It was dated Boston, October 20.

> "Just a line. I have changed my address and I have changed my name. From now on the name here will be Howard Thurston. And Julian, don't write me any more letters here as it looks bad – letters coming from the Island – as the mail man gets it and those at the Post Office look it over.
>
> I will get a box at the Post Office or I will have you send my mail to Montreal and then they can send it to me here, in another envelope.
>
> I had a letter from some lawyer named Gauvin and I could not read it. Julian, I want you to let me know what is going on in regard to the *Columba*. And as far as Lepine is concerned I don't care who takes care of my interest as long as you see that I am protected, only I don't want two or three lawyers looking after it as it will run into a lot of expense.

You can send any letters to Howard Thurston, Room 910, Canada Cement Building, Montreal.

Well Julian, I hope to get this off. We always seem to work on the moon and everyone else works in the dark. However, we must do the best we can.

As ever, your friend, J. J. H, Jr.

PS: Julian, let me know what code to use so I can correspond with you easier."

The "J. J. H., Jr" stood for J. J. Healey, Jr., undoubtedly fictitious as there were other letters signed J. J. Murdock. (Henri Moraze, St. Pierre, supplied this example of a letter typical of the times.)

Only weeks after the writing of the above, the required majority of states had approved the end of Prohibition, and the Twenty-First Amendment became a thing of the past on December 3. The Depression had exerted perhaps the greatest influence on repeal, along with the Democrats making it part of their election plank the previous year, and Franklin Roosevelt sealed the ultimate doom of the Volstead Act when he spoke at his party's nominating convention. The name of Andrew Volstead had somewhat unfairly been vilified in the minds of the American people and the history books. It was Volstead's intention to hit the saloons without jeopardizing citizens' rights to consume alcohol in their homes. Other hands had intervened to produce the total ban on what they considered the "demon rum."

Prohibition enriched organized crime in the United States, even as it failed in its other aims. Enforcement of the Volstead Act became a nightmare, more resembling a sort of organized warfare than ordinary policing on a large scale. When the end came, few law-abiding citizens regretted the passing of the speakeasies and the violence, epitomized by the likes of "Legs" Diamond, Al Capone, Meyer Lansky, and a host of others whose names were household words during the "dry" era.

During this period, St. Pierre stood as a rocky bastion in the Atlantic, profiting from its perfectly legal middleman role. The tiny fraction of the profits from the trade that accrued to the local authorities was still sufficient to complete important improvements to the infrastructure of the town, but the big money was held firmly within the grasp of the Canadian distillers and those on the other end of the chain who supplied the thirsty American drinking public.

With repeal came a winding down of St. Pierre's involvement with the liquor trade, though there were scores to settle in distilling and government circles. Henry Morgenthau, Jr., American Secretary of the Treasury, did some figuring and decided that Canada's distilleries owed some $60,000,000 in excise and customs tariffs evaded by operators along Rum Row and in the transborder traffic. He held a trump card, in announcing the possibilities of a ban on legal imports from Canada until the bill could be marked paid. Secretary of State Cordell Hull handled the negotiations for the American Government, and in due time, while Canadian distillers stewed in apprehension, a lesser, "ballpark" figure of five per cent was declared acceptable and whisky began to flow across the border from the huge stocks on hand in bonded warehouses of the Dominion.

At a stroke, repeal removed a score of problems that had plagued the U.S.A. ever since the Volstead Act was passed. In St. Pierre, it left the populace facing a future uncertain, but probably bleak. For a decade and a half, while the rest of the world suffered through the worst Depression it had ever known, life on the island colony of St. Pierre and Miquelon had been exciting, prosperous, and replete with onshore jobs. The old ways of fishing for a living had largely been forgotten, and there was little enthusiasm for the return to the time-honoured paths of life. Repeal cut both ways; in Canada and especially the United States it was a relief, even a blessing. In St. Pierre, the future appeared cheerless.

On the day that Prohibition ended, the truckers who had been engaged in transporting the liquor shipments from the docks to the warehouses and vice versa organized a mock funeral parade from one of the liquor warehouses. They paraded throughout the community with a long line of trucks, with the American and French flags at half-mast in mourning, signifying that the great era was all over and tomorrow they would have no more work.

End of Prohibition, December 1933 – truckers parade with American and French flags at half-mast in mourning.
(Photo courtesy of Briand-Ozon collection)

THE *KROMHOUT* INCIDENT

Prohibition in the U.S. was finally over. The huge traffic from St. Pierre to the States would quickly come to an end. Such was not the case with Canada and Newfoundland, where the traffic would still go on for a certain period.

Repeal of Prohibition was only hours old when an incident took place in Canadian waters that, while it had some unusual aspects, well illustrates the nature of the work of the Preventive Service and its interaction with rumrunners. Far different from ordinary piracy, the *"Kromhout* Incident" resulted in charges of a captain stealing his own ship and its cargo.

The story was recalled by Milton McKenzie, a resident of North Sydney, Nova Scotia, and one-time chief officer of the Preventive Service cutter *Stumble Inn,* also known as *Number 4.*

The other lead role in the drama was played by the Lunenburg-registered schooner *Kromhout.* Owned by a number of share-holders, she had been given her name after a deal with the Scandinavian manufacturer of her Kromhout engines, to help in advertising their value to the trade.

When this story began, the *Kromhout,* with 1,500 barrels of rum from St. Pierre as her cargo, was about seven miles off Flint Island, Cape Breton Island. Because the ship was of Canadian registry, Preventive Service officers could legally board and inspect her within the twelve-mile limit. Had she been foreign-registered, this could take place only within the three-mile limit.

Number 4 approached the *Kromhout* in darkness on a December morning in 1933. The rumrunner, surprised, turned and fled, pursued by the cutter whose "bow chasers" barked repeatedly. Finally, after a long chase, the *Kromhout* was following at the end of 700 feet of line.

Suddenly the tow line parted, apparently cut by someone, and the rumrunner immediately swung about and dashed for the open sea. The police ship followed, but kept falling farther behind. Gunfire to stop the *Kromhout* was ruled out because the police boat's prize crew was aboard: Chief Officer Milton McKenzie, Second Engineer James McIntosh, and Able Seamen Raymond Oxford and Murdock McDonald.

With her superior speed, the *Kromhout* soon was out of sight, with her valuable cargo and hostages. Within a few hours all available craft of Canada's Preventive Service had taken up the hunt and wireless messages were sent to shipping in the area to be on the lookout for her. However, none spotted the rumrunner, and she made port in St. Pierre, where the French authorities took a hand in the matter.

The governor of St. Pierre had been advised from Ottawa to be on the watch for the *Kromhout*. The cable having been written in English, there was a matter of translation to be handled; the governor, unfamiliar with English, handed it to an aide for translation. The word "detain" was interpreted to mean "jail," though the Department of External Affairs in Ottawa had actually requested that the vessel simply be held in St. Pierre.

The governor acted immediately, in the manner of a good neighbour, and he arrested the Lunenburg crew and lodged them behind bars. They were: Ross Mason, Master; Fred Acker, Mate; and Arthur Nickle, Lorrain Mason, Wallace Greek, Fred Tanner, Wilbert Greek, and Jessen Morash. The four policemen were comfortably accommodated after their long ordeal and soon were on their way to Nova Scotia aboard the Furness Red Cross Line steamer *Rosalind*.

The St. Pierre merchant who had supplied the *Kromhout*'s cargo was permitted to visit Captain Mason in jail. A wire was soon dispatched to the vessel's owners, and the latter quickly complained to Ottawa that the Canadian crew had been locked in small, dark cells. After receipt of a further cable from Ottawa, the embarrassed St. Pierre authorities released the seamen. Legal steps were quickly set in motion by Ottawa, seeking extradition of the crew and the return of the hijacked *Kromhout*.

The St. Pierre merchant who had owned the cargo, but who had not been fully paid, talked to his friend Captain Mason and suggested a way out of the mess; if the St. Pierre man lodged a lien against his unpaid goods, as a French citizen his lien would take legal priority over any other action, and he could have the vessel auctioned for the amount owing. A third party could purchase her for a nominal sum and restore the *Kromhout* to her Lunenburg owners. Captain Mason expressed confidence that the Preventive Service authorities would be unable to win a case against him as they would not be able to prove their position off Cape Breton Island. The Canadian cutter arrived in St. Pierre a few days later and took the *Kromhout* in tow, plus her crew, and headed back to Nova Scotia. The captain and crew agreed to return to Canada, of their own free will.

In mid-January, a preliminary hearing opened in police court in Halifax. The charges against the captain and crew of seven were for theft and aiding in theft. Evidence given the first day alleged that Captain Mason had shoved an RCMP constable away from the wheel of the seized craft and steered her away from her captor. He was said to have warned the police not to interfere or it would be "too bad for them." Three witnesses were heard that first day. They were W. J. Rowe, famous designer of the racing schooner *Bluenose*, First Officer McKenzie of the Preventive Service patrol boat *Number 4*, and Able Seaman Roberts. In charge of the prosecution was Gordon M. L. Daley, KC.

Seaman Roberts, drawing upon twenty years of seagoing experience, was definite that the tow rope had been cut. First Officer McKenzie denied that he had had anything to do with it. Three separate breaks in the rope figured in the tangled evidence. The courtroom almost resembled a schoolroom in navigation, with nautical terms constantly bandied by witnesses and lawyers. The seamen were defended by W. Pitt Potter, of Lunenburg.

Mr. McKenzie testified that on December 6 he had come on watch at four in the morning. The weather was cloudy, a moderate wind was blowing, and the light swell was increasing. "I patrolled west-southwest and steamed the log at zero. The patrol boat had two engines of 180 horsepower each," he told the court.

"We proceeded on course at cruising speed until 4:35 a.m., when Captain Hyson called me to his cabin to inquire about the weather. Speed was reduced until 6:55 a.m. when a vessel was sighted. The *Number 4* hailed the *Kromhout* and put off a dory with a boarding party, but as the dory started away from the ship, the *Kromhout* headed off. The cutter followed the *Kromhout* for a couple of miles but had to return to pick up the dory crew.

Between ten-thirty and eleven o'clock, the witness went on watch again and observed the rumrunner seven or eight miles ahead. Eventually, she was overtaken. "We ran up the three-flag signal to heave to, but she paid no attention until we came along-side. Then she stopped," McKenzie told the court.

"When I went on board, I went aft to see the captain and inspect his papers. When asked for a manifest, Mason replied, 'I haven't any.'" McKenzie asked, "What are you loaded with?" and Mason replied, "Just a little booze."

Captain Hyson then arrived on board and said to Captain Mason, "I seize this vessel in the name of His Majesty."

Mason replied, "You can't do that, she's on the high seas," to which the Preventive Service officer grimly responded, "We'll let the future look after that."

By this time, a tow line had been hauled aboard the *Kromhout* and made fast, and tow got under way, with only the *Kromhout*'s foresail set. Owing to the heavy swell, and a short line, the tow line parted. Captain Hyson shouted to his men aboard the rumrunner to hoist the other sails and sail the vessel to port. Mason warned his crew not to assist the cutter's party.

In an effort to speed up the operation, a second tow line was placed aboard, and soon it also parted. Finally, Captain Hyson passed a third line, a three-and-a-half-inch new manila hawser, and this was secured at about two-thirty. Evidence was presented that this line had been securely fastened, but it also subsequently parted under unexplained circumstances.

Captain Mason went below just before the ships entered "Main a Dieu Passage." A little later the mate arrived on deck to say the captain wanted the jib set; Mason was reported to have "had a few under his belt." The mate ordered the jib set, and the crew responded in oilskins.

After the jib was raised, Mr. McKenzie told the court Seaman McDonald took the wheel, and while McKenzie was walking up and down, he heard the engine start. Captain Mason arrived on deck and, according to McDonald, shoved him from the wheel and ordered a course set toward the east. McKenzie testified that he told his men to go below and let the future take its course. The first land sighted was at five o'clock the following afternoon. The *Kromhout* continued to St. Pierre Harbour. All members of the vessel's crew, except Tanner, had taken turns working the ship.

Under questioning by Mr. Potter, for the defence, McKenzie admitted that he had no accurate evidence to show that the *Kromhout* was within the twelve-mile limit when first sighted, other than a "dead reckoning" estimate. After Mason took the wheel, McKenzie and his men went below with no idea of where the ship was bound.

> Question: "Why didn't you ask Captain Mason to set a course for Sydney?"
>
> Answer: "I wasn't taking any chances of being knocked over the side."

McKenzie admitted that he had a thirty-eight-calibre revolver in a holster and that no one had tried to take it from him. He had placed it under a mattress as they neared St. Pierre. He saw no other firearms aboard *Kromhout*.

Question: "You made no effort to take charge of the vessel?"

Answer: "Not after he told me to get away, and jumped and kicked like an old fool."

McKenzie told the court he had been given good treatment on the *Kromhout*.

In explanation of why he had sought to hide his revolver under a mattress, McKenzie said he had never been in St. Pierre and didn't know if one was allowed to carry firearms. Answering a further question by Mr. Daley as to why he failed to use his revolver, McKenzie answered that "it would give people more chance to talk about the brutality of the RCMP with guns."

After a heated debate with the defence counsel, Mr. Daley told the court he would proceed under Section 207 of the Customs Act, relating to hovering in territorial waters with a contraband cargo.

The following day Captain Hyson was on the stand, giving evidence similar to that of Mr. McKenzie. He was questioned by Mr. Potter.

Potter: "Can you indicate any offence this vessel had committed, or you suspected she had committed, when you attempted to bring her in?"

Hyson: "I suspected she had contraband and she was hovering."

Captain Hyson said he didn't recall Captain Mason saying he was forty miles off shore when Hyson came aboard. He also couldn't swear he had not told Captain Mason he had orders from Ottawa to take him in, but he thought he had said he possessed "orders from headquarters."

Question: "Do you remember Mate Acker saying 'You must think we're children to go inside the twelve-mile limit so you can seize this vessel'?" The witness replied that he had heard something to that effect.

The case lumbered on, and eventually reached the Supreme Court, with the rumrunner losing. Prime evidence was a map, found by police behind some furniture, showing the position of the *Kromhout*, and that cinched the case. Without the map there might have been a different result.

Captain Mason was sentenced to three years in Dorchester Penitentiary on each of three counts: theft of his own ship, theft of its liquor cargo, and resisting a police officer. The sentences were to run concurrently. Mr. Justice Doull commented that the offences were serious ones and required severe penalties. Mason accepted the judgment of the court without apparent emotion.

What about the *Kromhout*? She remained tied up for a lengthy period and eventually was sold to Churchill's, of Bay Roberts, Newfoundland. For several years thereafter she served as a coastal freighter.

According to a St. Pierre man who remembers the incident, the *Kromhout* should never have been caught by the *Stumble Inn*. Her crew was far under the weather with alcohol and incapable of good navigation, and she was away off course, near the Cape Breton shore. At the time, she should have been off Halifax for a rendezvous with ships that were patiently awaiting her appearance.

The case of the *Kromhout*, recorded here in some detail, was not unlike the fate of many another rumrunner caught in Canadian or American waters. The Canadian Preventive Service rarely enforced the laws by gunfire; however, off American shores, with the involvement of the gangster element throughout the latter days of Prohibition, violence and the free use of weapons was the name of the game.

The *Kromhout,* which headed to St. Pierre having on board the **RCMP** boarding crew. **Her captain was sentenced to three years in jail at Dorchester Penitentiary for this incident.** (Photo courtesy of Captain R. C. Butt)

POSTSCRIPT TO PROHIBITION

The end of the Volstead Act in the U.S. didn't signal the conclusion of the liquor traffic in St. Pierre, though it saw a winding down of the sort of operations that had come to be regarded as almost normal. The ultimate blow to the St. Pierre economy was still to come, from the hands of the Government of France, in April of 1935.

There remained for some time, in 1934, a brisk trade with Canadian coastal points and the St. Lawrence River area. Liquor at bargain prices held a strong appeal for customers in Prince Edward Island, New Brunswick, points along the Quebec shore, and in nearby Newfoundland. This business was of long standing, and the very idea of Canadian-produced liquor being exported to St. Pierre and then returned surreptitiously without payment of customs and excise duties bothered the Conservative government headed by Prime Minister Richard B. Bennett. Bennett had ousted Mackenzie King in 1930. In opposition, he had constantly hounded King for not acting on the recommendations of a Royal Commission to proceed with an all-out prosecution of the Bronfmans for their role in the business. Harry Bronfman had been tried in Saskatchewan for his activities in the prairie provinces, but there was still the St. Pierre connection. Now that Bennett was in power, he was determined to launch a full investigation into the offshore smuggling business, including the laundering of profits earned in St. Pierre.

Late in 1934, charges were laid against the four Bronfmans and

Barney Aaron, their brother-in-law, plus sixty-five others alleged to have manoeuvred the government out of the tax revenues.

The trial opened in Montreal in January 1935, and lasted until mid-June. Corporate bank accounts of Atlas Shipping Co., owned by the Bronfmans and listed as simultaneously domiciled in St. Pierre, Bermuda, Saint John, and Belize, were brought into court for scrutiny. It was revealed that during the preceding twelve months, $3,055,166 had been transferred from the shipping company's St. Pierre operation to the "Brintcan" account, a Bronfman family holding company. Atlas Shipping's Halifax office was in charge of chartering boats for the smuggling trade, as many as forty at one time.

The government's case ran into almost insurmountable difficulties when the Royal Canadian Mounted Police raided the head office of Seagram's to get the Atlas and Brintcan books of account. The search turned up nothing of use, and the courtroom was treated to stories of burlap sacks of documents spirited out of the offices and burned in the cellar of a private home. Perhaps the most colourful witness was "Big Fred" Levesque, captain of smuggling vessels in the Gulf of St. Lawrence. On one voyage he had been skipper of the barge *Tremblay* on a run from St. Pierre to Rivière-du-Loup. During the trip he had noticed about 1,000 gallons of his cargo turning rusty in the cast iron drums. Asked by Judge Jules Desmarais if he had been reimbursed for the rusty alcohol, Levesque replied that he had not, that "Abe Bronfman told me to filter it though a loaf of bread."

The defendants had been charged with "conspiring to violate the statues of a friendly country," a euphemism for smuggling, but close questioning by the defence lawyers revealed that the Crown was, in fact, unable to prove to the judge's satisfaction that smuggling had actually taken place. The prosecutor contended that the bank records showed that large amounts had been transferred from Atlas Shipping's St. Pierre account for the purpose of smuggling into both Canada and the United States, but despite the Crown's best efforts to connect the defendants with smuggling, Judge Desmarais rendered a not guilty verdict on June 15. Part of his judgment read:

"The Crown claims that the accused opened agencies in Newfoundland and St. Pierre et Miquelon that were useless for any purpose other than smuggling and that sales made there to Canadians constitutes proof of illegal conspiracy, yet the accused had every legal right to organize these agencies in the interests of their business. It does not appear in the evidence that the accused did anything whatever to assist in importing liquor into Canada and the accused are herewith discharged."

So much for allegations as compared with proof! The defendants smiled broadly, but the RCMP were less than happy. Following the verdict they subpoenaed Judge Desmarais's bank records and checked his safety deposit box. No incriminating evidence was found.

At the end of Prohibition, and while the Montreal trial was taking place, operators in St. Pierre and along the coast of Newfoundland were endeavouring to turn rumrunning boats into cash. The vessels were put on the market by ship brokers who managed them for the syndicates. Illustrative of dealings for these craft is a letter dated October 25, 1934, from W. Lawrence Sweeney, ship broker of Yarmouth, Nova Scotia, to Julien Moraze of St. Pierre:

"The motor vessel *Reo I* is owned by Berky Cravitz, and George Morrel, of Digby, N.S., is looking after her. I understand the price asked for her is $7,000. She is not a bargain at that price.

The *Reo II* is under seizure at Havana, Cuba. I doubt if she will return north.

Harris Himmelman at Lunenburg owns the *Shogomac* which can be bought for less than $6,500. The *Beatrice L* can be bought for around $8,000. The *Shananlian* can be bought for $15,000.

There are a number of other boats here which can be bought such as the *Connoisseur, Ann D, Apohaqui, Placentia, Tatamagouche, Accuracy,* etc and should any one be of interest to you I no doubt can secure full particulars from the agents of the owners."

Many of these vessels ended their days as coasters in Newfoundland waters.

There is evidence of perhaps some undue haste on the part of owners to dispose of their boats. Another letter, just two months later and written aboard a ship of the Eastern Steamship Line, also from Mr. Sweeney to Julien Moraze, gives a different picture of the situation. Dated December 5, 1934, it reads:

"Received your letter and regret very much the quoted prices were too high.

A few months ago one could secure practically any boat at a bargain, but today things are changed as a great many of the boats are working and the owners are making money, so therefore will not sell unless they get a good price.

The *Beatrice L* is owned by Bernard Melanson, of Gilbert's Cove, Digby Co. He paid for her $7,250 and at the present time is offering her for sale at $8,000.

Tom Cogger, of Saint John, N.B., has the *Glomacan* and I believe would sell her.

The *Beatrice L* engine is perfect.

The *Popocatapeldt* could have been bought for $9,000. She is also perfect."

There were still some stocks of Canadian distilled rye and bourbon in the warehouses. These were almost all in pint bottles. In preparation for their exit from the islands, the big Canadian distilleries sent empty barrels to the island and all remaining stocks were ordered to be transferred into the barrels. These were to be sent back to the distillery for blending and to be bottled and labelled with post-Prohibition brands. All of the old brands were no longer legal, as they contained names like Peter Pan, Four Aces, Coon Hollow, etc.

All these now embarrassing bottles were ordered to be destroyed. Many were taken by lighters and sunk in what was at the time deep water. The divers of the era were very limited as to the depth which they could go down.

When I was originally researching this book in the 1970s, one of the gentlemen who worked in the warehouses told me the story of these bottles and showed me on a map the areas where they had been submerged.

By the 1990s, diving techniques had evolved considerably and depths were no longer a problem. A diver friend volunteered to search, and after a number of dives was successful in retrieving numerous beautifully engraved whisky bottles that had spent more than sixty years submerged. They have been preserved and are exhibited at the Hotel Robert in St. Pierre, along with other Prohibition memorabilia.

Despite some "trips south" and the traffic to the Gulf of St. Lawrence, the trade was winding down in St. Pierre. More than a year after the end of Prohibition, France bowed to pressure from the U.S. Government to put a halt to the liquor shipping business in St. Pierre. As of April 9, 1935, shippers of alcoholic products from St. Pierre were required to post a bond guaranteeing that the goods would reach destinations shown on the manifests. The decree raised a storm of protest in St. Pierre, but to no avail, and the island's days of importance to the liquor trade had come to an end. However, it was ironic that the death knell in St. Pierre had tolled in Paris. Foreign companies began burning papers and packing up to leave town, the Canadian Bank of Commerce disposed of its banking business, and the large-scale rumrunning days were just about over.

Henri Moraze was a keen businessman, and if this was going to be the law, he would find a way around it.

He felt that he could purchase a boat in Europe that could hold

Henri Moraze was a leading merchant involved in the liquor trade during and after Prohibition in Atlantic Canada and Quebec.
(Photo courtesy of Mr. Gustave Roblot)

10,000 cases. He would load his alcohol directly in Europe and come back to a position just outside the territorial limit of St. Pierre, and remain in international waters. He would send his motorboats to the mother vessel, and they would load up prior to going up the Gulf of St. Lawrence.

The freight from Europe to St. Pierre on a case of alcohol was $0.45 a case, for a total cost of $0.85 per case. With 10,000 cases, this would make $8,100. Within two trips the vessel and expenses would be paid for.

After repeal came about, there was a definite desire by the U.S. to put a stop to this practice of the liquor trade.

Promises were made by the U.S. that there would be new legislation enacted, granting the President the possibility of concluding commercial treaties and consenting to lower customs duties on certain goods to collaborating countries.

Having seen these possibilities, French authorities proposed to Washington the opening of official negotiations.

Without forewarning, France swiftly passed a decree. In April of 1935, lower customs tariffs to the U.S. were more appealing than a few thousand cases of alcohol that in any event weren't destined to the U.S., but to Canada.

Henri Moraze was up in arms. He advised the minister of colonies in Paris that this decree would be the decimation of the old colony of St. Pierre and Miquelon.

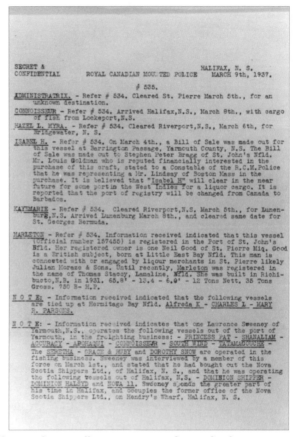

The RCMP kept tabs on all movements of vessels that were or had been involved in the rumrunning trade. (Author collection)

During the Prohibition era, St. Pierre had had years of prosperity from the importation of hundreds of thousands of cases of alcohol, which had a small import duty. From this prosperity cash reserves were accumulated, but the largest part of this reserve was used in some work projects, such as the building of a modern harbour, the upgrading of all government buildings, making new roads, and water and sewer work.

Moraze stated, "We were proud of our little island, to show its tri-colour, and proud to present to visitors to the islands the last vestiges of France in North America, which were now in excellent shape.

"I take the liberty to bring to your attention, of the grave consequences of such a measure, which will be the ruination of old dear colony.

"I would ask you before making such a decision, to back away from it for as long as you can, to give all the local merchants time to clear their stocks."

There was no such delay, and it was announced that alcohol could only be shipped in vessels of 200 or more tons, and that no customs clearance for the high seas would be delivered, as had been done previously. It was now necessary to indicate the country of destination. A bond of fifteen francs per litre of alcohol was to be given to French customs, and this would only be cancelled once a certificate of landing was obtained from the destination country.

A member of the National Assembly, Mr. Henry Fougere, took up the case and made a representation to the French Government, advising them that cash reserves of the colony accumulated during the Prohibition era had now dried up and that the new budget for the islands was now showing a deficit of 6,000,000 francs.

It was understood that in view of diplomatic representations of the U.S. Government, the French Government had agreed to take a decree, which was for reasons of national interests, but the way this decree was made was that it applied to all shipments, even those that were not destined to the U.S.

A request was made to amend the said decree, to limit its application only for goods destined to the U.S., which were in any case no longer existent.

Henri Moraze was worried: he had good cases of alcohol in his warehouse, 12,000 more cases arriving in a week, and another 12,000 cases arriving in a day; in all, 33,000 cases. A lot of money was tied up in this stock. This new law had been a surprise, and there had been no transition period to get rid of existing stock.

On a local scale, Moraze had made a lot of money during the

prohibition, and he wasn't about to let a new law put a stop to his business. His immediate problem was to find a way of getting rid of existing stocks. He had a Plan B, which was to purchase a vessel that could be used as a mother ship.

The local government on the islands proved reasonable and co-operative in the matter of letting the local merchants get rid of their stock of alcohol. They conveniently turned a blind eye when it was felt to be both politically and economically wise.

There were ways and means readily available. St. Pierre's electrical generating system shut down at midnight, and the ensuing darkness made it easy for small vessels to load at the outer wharves. Trucks without lights would move liquor from warehouses to docks. On especially black nights, a trail of fishery salt served to show the centre line on roadways. On one of the docks there was a small lighthouse; to avoid detection by a beam from this light, some burlap bags were stowed close at hand to cover the lamp.

St. Pierre customs officers checked purchases of gasoline as possible evidence of lengthy trips and illegal activities. Boatmen soon learned to take aboard only small quantities in St. Pierre, enough to get them to a pre-arranged rendezvous with a fisherman from Burin on the nearby Newfoundland shore. The Newfoundlanders were co-operative in supplying fuel enough for delivery trips to points in the Gulf of St. Lawrence.

Trade continued relatively briskly while warehouses were being emptied and merchants' stocks reduced. Henri Moraze had been inquiring about the availability and prices for former rumrunners. He had studied the system and soon devised a way to beat it. Not finding what he wanted among the heavily engined rumrunners for sale in Nova Scotia, he purchased a Scandinavian three-master of steel construction, the *Grete Kure*. She was registered in St. John's, Newfoundland, and never officially came within St. Pierre's three-mile limit. However, as a foreign-registered vessel, she could seek shelter from storms in the island's harbour.

The vessel was equipped with a wireless, and a few days before arriving on location, coded messages would be sent so that his rumrunning vessels and other clients could come alongside the mother vessel. He was positive that he could still make a lot money.

However, the RCMP patrol fleet, along with constantly improving shore communications, increasingly made rumrunning far from prosperous; the days of big money were gone, and so were the days of rumrunning to Canada.

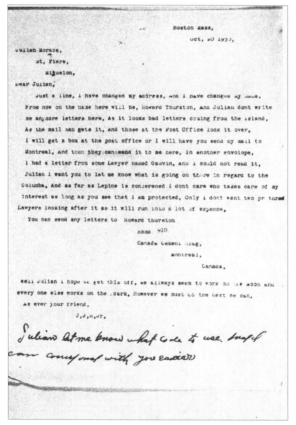

Letter from an American rumrunner to Henri Moraze of St. Pierre stating: "I have changed my name and my address."
(Document courtesy of Mr. Henri Moraze)

Canadian Coast Guard cutter patrolling in the Gulf of St. Lawrence.
(Photo courtesy of Captain Milton Mackenzie)

The *Liberty Newfoundland*, owned by Henri Moraze of St. Pierre, registered a high speed. (Photo courtesy of Captain R. C. Butt)

A shipment of tins of pure alcohol seized by the Canadian cutter _Alachasse_ off Nova Scotia. (Photo courtesy of Captain R. C. Butt)

Barrels of rum seized by cutters in Gulf of St. Lawrence.
(Photo courtesy of the RCMP Archives)

A small landing craft being torched in St. Lawrence River to destroy evidence.
(Photo courtesy of the RCMP Archives)

**The RCMP started to use a seaplane in the Gulf of St. Lawrence
to position the whereabouts of rumrunners.**
(Photo courtesy of Mrs. Marie Enguehard)

RCMP seaplane in Cheticamp, Nova Scotia.
(Author collection)

Grete Kure – a Scandinavian vessel to transport and store alcohol in international waters off St. Pierre after the French Government no longer issued clearances for the high seas in 1930. (Photo courtesy of Briand-Ozon collection)

Rumrunning schooner *May + June*, registered in Newfoundland but actually owned by Henri Moraze of St. Pierre. (Photo courtesy of Captain R. C. Butt)

Two Newfoundlanders, Keeping and Stoodley, on deck of rumrunning schooner *May and June*, which was owned by Henri Moraze of St. Pierre but registered in NL. (Author collection)

Rumrunning schooners *Charles L* owned by Petite's of English Harbour West, and *Helen G MacLean* owned by Henri Moraze of St. Pierre transferring rum on Burgeo Bank. (Photo courtesy of Captain R. C. Butt)

It was a short hop for boats from Newfoundland with high-powered engines to cross over to St. Pierre for a load of spirits and tobacco. (Author collection)

NEWFOUNDLAND RUMRUNNING

Newfoundlanders were from the earliest times bartering with St. Pierre residents products such as billets (logs cut up for firewood), spruce boughs to make a non-alcoholic spruce beer, partridge, lobster, salmon, and clams. Hand-knitted wool socks, bakeapples, etc. would be traded for black rum.

However, back before the days of confederation with Canada, Newfoundlanders who had access to St. Pierre were known to smuggle home food from the island. Flour, tea, molasses, sugar, and other supplies were readily available at a much lower cost than one had to pay in Newfoundland. One hundred pounds of sugar went for $3.00, while the Newfoundland price was $10.00. Cigarettes were sold in St. Pierre for $0.02 a pack and a ten-gallon keg of rum cost only $10.00. From this we can see why it was attractive to deal with the French Islands.

It was common practice in those days to go to St. Pierre to pick up whatever supplies were needed, hide them under the fish that was caught during the day and make way for the nearest uninhabited island to stash the goods until dark. In many cases, it was Morgan's Island, named after the notorious pirate Captain Morgan who is supposed to have buried some of his ill-gotten treasure there.

Back then the Newfoundland Ranger force was carrying out patrols in the area. Customs officers were all over the place looking out for loads of contraband. If they caught anybody they forced them to pay duty charges on the goods.

Smuggling liquor and tobacco products by south coast fishermen in those days took place regularly, mostly for the consumption of the runners themselves as well as their families and friends. There was not wide-scale distribution.

Rumours have it that, many years ago on the south coast of Newfoundland, there was a good team looking after infractions in the liquor trade. It consisted of a customs official who made his best attempts to catch the rumrunners and seize their liquid cargo, and a magistrate who would render judgment on these colourful, so-called "illegal activities." It was said that both the customs official and the judge were alcoholics, who more often than anyone else were intoxicated.

When the customs official chased the rumrunners and made the seizure, the bottles involved would be stored in the basement of a school. It was said that it would take upward to six months for the case to be heard and for judgment to be rendered. As always, the confiscated goods were ordered destroyed by the magistrate. During the long months of storage, the contents of the bottles would mysteriously disappear and be substituted with tea. Thank goodness it hadn't been lost for everyone.

By the time the Second World War started in 1939, rumrunning operations from St. Pierre to the rest of the Maritimes and Quebec came to an end. Enforcement methods had improved significantly, and due to the distances involved, it was too risky to try to bring larger vessels close to the Canadian shores, where they were subject to confiscation. Only Newfoundland fishermen persisted, in their small dories. It was difficult to patrol the long Newfoundland coastline with its proximity to the French Islands. The fishermen in any case were willing to take the risk.

In fact, ever since there had been a duty, there had been a person known as a smuggler. Residents of the Burin Peninsula had the advantage of having St. Pierre, known locally at that time as St. Peter's, a mere twelve miles from the top of the peninsula. Of course, that wasn't to say that they were all involved in smuggling, but in any group there are always a few who will try to beat the system, no matter what the odds.

Newfoundland joined Canada on March 31, 1949. The Royal Canadian Mounted Police were to take over policing activities on the island from the Newfoundland Rangers on August 1, 1950, with the exception of federal statutes relating to customs and excise statutes, as well as the drug act.

The RCMP immediately became involved with the rumrunners on the Burin Peninsula and the south coast.

Establishing a police force in a newly acquired province such as Newfoundland was bound to present challenges. The harmonizing of Canadian laws with those of Newfoundland was not an easy task; however, the task was softened through interpretation and application because many Newfoundland lawyers were graduates of Dalhousie University and found the Canadian legal system less cumbersome than their own.

Neither the RCMP nor other branches of Canadian Government were given the warmth of royal treatment in this new province, where confederation with Canada had won by such a narrow margin. Many Newfoundlanders were afraid of the whole business of Confederation, and in April 1949, some houses had black crepe on the doors and black flags flying.

It was against this frame of mind that the RCMP established their policing duties on the Burin Peninsula, where rumrunning was a tradition from grandfather to father to son, and where smuggling a few bottles of rum for a wedding, Christmas, or for your neighbours was certainly not considered a crime. Nevertheless, the law was the law and the RCMP had to enforce it.

In the early 1950s, there were only two ways of getting liquor on the Burin Peninsula: you either ordered it from St. John's, or you would get it from St. Pierre. Entire communities would often pool their funds together and send a couple of men to St. Pierre to pick up the desired liquor supplies.

In some communities, though, there was an official resentment against alcohol. In November 1954, the Temperance Society held sessions in the Temperance Hall, where members were told of the evils and damaging effects of alcohol. It stressed the vital importance of children and youth being taught the nature and negative effects of liquor as a beverage.

A divine service was held at the United Church when the Rev. Edward Morris delivered a thought-provoking and impressive seminar on Temperance and Christian faith to a very large congregation.

Unofficially, many enjoyed a drink and went about procuring it.

In the fall of 1954, a large seizure of liquor was made by the RCMP near Lawn, Newfoundland, where they apprehended two dories bringing liquor ashore. Both dories and the liquor were confiscated by the authorities. Court action followed where ten residents of Lawn were fined a total of $2,000 or two years in the penitentiary for breaches of the Alcoholic Liquors Act.

It was understood that several of the accused were to serve their sentences instead of paying their fines.

* * *

With the arrival of the RCMP on the peninsula, new methods were used to track rumrunners. In fact, sometimes the work of the RCMP in Newfoundland went to the dogs – or at least a dog. The RCMP at times called upon the services of a German shepherd. Bruce was one such highly trained police dog.

In Grand Bank, Bruce succeeded in leading his master to a large quantity of smuggled liquor which was hidden in the woods.

In early 1955, charges were flying that there was a ring in St. John's hauling smuggled liquor from St. Pierre.

These facts were strongly denied by Michel Moreux, the French consul in St. John's, who stated that he had no report from the governor of St. Pierre or the RCMP of any widespread smuggling wave.

A few fishermen, he said, had been known to smuggle rum from the islands, but it was for their own consumption and not for widespread distribution. None of it was making its way to St. John's, for instance.

Both the RCMP and the French consul in St. John's believed that it was likely that St. Pierre Liquor made its way to St. John's for wholesale selling, especially since the foreign seamen who came to St. John's were willing and able to sell their supplies. There were so many foreign vessels in port that, in spite of patrolling the waterfront, the RCMP had difficulties in deterring the Spanish, Portuguese, and other foreign seamen from bringing ashore liquor that had not been declared to customs officials.

In those days smuggled goods under the value of $200 would bring a relatively light fine, while goods valued over that had a heavier consequence.

In May of 1955, members of the RCMP detachment in St. Lawrence seized a total of forty-five gallons of pure alcohol in that community. They raided the launch of a travelling salesman after he returned from St. Pierre.

On a much smaller scale, but typical of the era when liquor was not readily available on the peninsula, two residents of St. Lawrence, getting off the ferry from St. Pierre, were apprehended and searched by local RCMP officers. They were found to have in their possession thirteen bottles of contraband liquor. In court they were fined $100 by Magistrate Jones.

The Mounties had been cracking down on visitors that had gone to St. Pierre and were attempting to bring back with them more liquor than they were legally allowed.

At the end of July 1955, one of the largest seizures of contraband liquor for some time on the Burin Peninsula was made when members of the Grand Bank detachment of the RCMP conducted a raid in Lorries.

Two hundred bottles of assorted liquor as well as 435 gallons of pure white alcohol were included in their seizure.

The dory in which it is alleged the smuggled goods were transported from St. Pierre to Lorries was seized, and charges were laid against two or more men of the settlement. The value of the seized contraband liquor amounted to several thousand dollars.

The RCMP were going all-out to crack down on smugglers on Newfoundland's south coast, and kept at least one patrol vessel on the prowl between the French Islands and the Newfoundland shore-line.

Most of the contraband goods were shipped to the Newfoundland shore at night in dories. When they spotted the RCMP, it is known that fishermen would drop the liquor and alcohol in bags with salt that would later dissolve, causing the goods to float to the surface where it could be picked up safe from scrutiny. The presence of the RCMP resulted in a common gripe on the peninsula that the good old days were gone. They felt there was no sense to it anymore. The Mounties were always poking around, and they came right up to your door. Back in the old days, if you made it to your house, you were safe, but not so today in these times of warrants and summonses. This was the hard reality of Newfoundland being Canada's tenth province.

Although the tactics of customs officials and law enforcement officials had made smuggling much more difficult, it still went on. The rumrunners were still plying the waves in an effort to make a fast buck and keep their incomes at a reasonable level.

In the mid-1950s, the preferred drink on the south coast was pure white alcohol, also known as Alky. The alcohol was almost ninety-nine per cent pure. It was sold in two-and-a-half-gallon metal tins.

The smugglers carefully watched the whereabouts of the RCMP patrol vessel and made their move when they felt it was not nearby. Once landed, the contraband was often hidden in the woods, in the ground, or in homes.

Smuggled goods with a value of less than $200 would bring a relatively light fine if discovered, while over that amount had heavier consequences. When caught with larger quantities, some residents of the south coast opted to go to jail rather than pay the fine imposed by the judge.

Later in the fall of 1955, the RCMP cutter *Fort Walsh*, which had operated the south coast patrol, was replaced by another vessel, the *McBrien*.

At the end of April 1957, officers from the Grand Bank RCMP

detachment seized a quantity of rum in High Beach on the Burin Peninsula. They arrested a resident of the area for possession of contraband liquor.

In the fall of 1959, a Canadian-owned tanker arrived in Burgeo from St. Pierre. The RCMP raided the vessel and found a large quantity of assorted alcohol. The tanker had to pay a substantial fine prior to being released.

At the end of October 1959, RCMP officers from the St. Lawrence detachment received a tip that a quantity of contraband liquor had been brought ashore in their area. They searched the coastline and among the rocks they discovered a total of sixty gallons of alcohol and 100 bottles of rum. They tried to determine the owners of this contraband originating from neighbouring St. Pierre. At that time of the year, Christmas supplies were already being brought in. Both RCMP land officers and the marine patrol unit were doing their best to try and curb the trade.

At the end of June 1960, a dory with two men on board returning to the Burin Peninsula with an assorted load of liquor was overtaken by a southeast gale. With great difficulty the two men managed to get the dory safely to Morgan's Island. The dory was considerably damaged in the process. They spent the night on the island. Their signals were observed and they were rescued the next day.

The RCMP were suspicious, and later visited the isolated island. As they anticipated, they found a quantity of alcohol. Their investigation concluded with the arrest of the two men with smuggling charges.

In early November 1960, the RCMP arrested two men from Lawn with a doryload of contraband liquor. They were released on $300 bail and ordered to appear in court at a later date to answer to these smuggling charges.

The smuggling of spirits from St. Pierre to Newfoundland was considered something of a national pastime. In fact, there had been an occasion in previous years when a judge from the central district court had looked sorrowfully over his spectacles at a man he had just fined for a breach of the Customs Act. He observed that it should be a lesson to him. "Remember," said the judge, "there's no sin in smuggling unless you get caught."

For the handful that got caught, there were many that got away. Some of the most delightful stories of Newfoundland ingenuity are concerned with the methods employed at the time to deceive customs and police. No less ingenious were the methods used to conceal the illicit goods after they had been safely brought ashore on the Newfoundland side.

In those days, legitimate liquor was available only from major centres on the south coast. Residents could have ordered it from these centres. For purely good neighbourly reasons, they preferred to take it in from St. Pierre under the cover of darkness. There was at the time a tolerant attitude toward the so-called crime of smuggling.

In April of 1961, Magistrate Noseworthy fined two residents of Lorries $25.00 and $50.00 when they appeared in court in Grand Bank. The men had in their possession a quantity of liquor that had been smuggled in from St. Pierre.

In July of 1961, the RCMP played cat and mouse with a rumrunner in fog off St. Lawrence. Several shots had to be fired to bring the fleeing boat to a stop. The RCMP seized the liquor shipment that was on board. A few days later, several tins of pure white alcohol and an assortment of contraband liquor were discovered on a secluded beach on the Burin Peninsula.

The RCMP kept quite busy with the liquor trafficking, as at the end of July 1961, they seized a cache on a small island near Lord's Cove. The seizure consisted of thirteen bottles of rum, seventy bottles of champagne, and ten two-and-a-half-gallon tins of alcohol.

In November of 1961, in scenes that spoke of the old days of piracy, rumrunners were carrying doryloads of liquor from St. Pierre to the Burin Peninsula. They had ingeniously landed them on lonely spots along the shoreline. It was known to area residents that a large cargo had been safely landed and that the rumrunners had securely cached it away.

Others were less successful in mid-November 1961. RCMP officers assisted by the RCMP Marine Division made a large seizure of contraband liquor that was being transported by a dory. Two residents of Lorries were caught red-handed as they were about to land their precious cargo on a beach near Lamaline. Their cargo was of considerable value, with a full assortment of liquors and alcohol for the Christmas trade.

A few days later, another big haul of Christmas cheer contraband was made in Webber's Bay, near Lawn on the Burin Peninsula. The RCMP ambushed a dory that had just arrived from St. Pierre, and seized 157 bottles of rum, forty-five gallons of white alcohol in two-and-a-half-gallon tins, as well as three five-gallon barrels of rum.

The RCMP were doing their best to try and crack down on these illegal shipments, but the hard reality was that they were only intercepting a handful of the rumrunners that had been unfortunate enough to have been at the wrong place at the wrong time. They were, in their minds, only carrying on the traditions of other generations before them.

The lack of liquor stores on the Burin Peninsula in that era resulted in many trips made to either St. Pierre from the Burin Peninsula or to Miquelon from other south coast communities. Prior to the Christmas season, they would stock up on the contraband alcohol, when lucrative prices could be obtained from their thirsty customers.

In December of 1961, the RCMP seized another doryload of liquor near Lawn. A resident was arrested. He faced the court in St. Lawrence in February of 1962 and was found guilty and fined $500 or one year in jail for the offence.

On March 15, 1963, the RCMP cutter *Acadian* apprehended a dory with two Point au Gaul residents that had ten two-and-a-half-gallon tins of pure alcohol on board. When presented to the courts a few days later, they were convicted on smuggling charges and each given the option of paying a $150 fine or spending three months in jail.

In August of 1963, it wasn't a dory but an aircraft that had arrived from St. Pierre and landed on Bell Island in Conception Bay, Newfoundland. The pilot handed over fifteen gallons of pure alcohol to two men with instructions to deliver it to a Bell Island address. As they were wheeling it down the road in a crude handcart, they were intercepted by RCMP officers. Alleged to have been involved in this novel smuggling operation was a police officer from the Newfoundland Constabulary. He was immediately suspended from his functions.

Smuggling activities continued at the same pace throughout the rest of the 1960s, with the dories running back and forth from St. Pierre to the Burin Peninsula, and from Miquelon to the rest of the southwest coast.

* * *

True to tradition, the fall months were the busiest time of the year for the RCMP on the Burin Peninsula. Police reported the illegal entry of liquor from the nearby French Islands in the fall of 1970 as being on par with other years.

In a three-week period from October 15, 1970, three seizures were made by the Grand Bank RCMP in the Point May area.

An RCMP spokesman stated they had found ten gallons of rum buried in a bog less than 100 metres from the houses in Point May. Earlier that week two separate seizures had been made in the same bog, with eight twenty-five-ounce bottles of alcohol in the first raid, and twelve bottles of rum uncovered in the second search.

The contraband liquor was well-hidden. Some was underwater and some buried as far down as five feet.

Two other liquor seizures had been made in early October in Fortune. These activities were still going on in spite of three board of liquor control outlets having opened their doors to service the liquor requirements of the Burin Peninsula. There was by all appearances a good market for cheap St. Pierre liquor and alcohol for the Christmas trade.

Normally after Christmas, there was a slackening off in rumrunning operations from St. Pierre.

The RCMP, when questioned if overall rumrunning decreased in winter, responded that winter weather often precluded the possibilities of dories and the like engaging in the smuggling trade.

* * *

The fall of 1971 was no different than the previous year in the illegal liquor traffic from St. Pierre.

Members of the Grand Bank detachment of the RCMP made yet another seizure of twenty-one bottles of contraband liquor in a home in Fortune in mid-November. A few days later, on November 20, a seizure which was described as one of the largest in recent years was made half a mile from the beach in Point Howe on the tip of the Burin Peninsula. It was alleged that the cache of contraband was smuggled to the area from the nearby island of St. Pierre, a day or so previously. At the time of the seizure, four men were involved in transferring the liquor to a car from the woods, where the RCMP had been hidden not more than ten feet away from the transfer. When the RCMP made their presence known, they found some liquor in the car, while a quantity was still on the road and remained hidden in the bush alongside the vehicle. The seizure consisted of seventeen two-and-a-half-gallon tins of alcohol, twelve twenty-six-ounce bottles of rum, three forty-ounce bottles of rum, fifty-six jars of rum, and one case of wine.

In those days, when such a small quantity of liquor was considered a large seizure, laws were quite different than they are today. In that particular case, it was felt that if regular procedure was followed, a penalty would be assessed against the car. If the owner paid the penalty, the car would be released. If the penalty was not paid, it would be sold by the Crown. If the charges laid against the men ended up in a guilty verdict, the four men would each have to pay fines ranging from $200 to $1,000.

The RCMP said the seized liquor was purchased in St. Pierre for

$450 to $500. If the contraband had found its way on the local market, it would have fetched about $2,000.

In early September of 1974, the RCMP patrol vessel *Standoff* came upon and seized a fifty-five-foot-long vessel called the *Elizabeth Joanne*, from Rose Blanche, a small community on the province's southwest coast.

The longliner with eight men aboard was en route to Rose Blanche when she was apprehended by the patrol vessel and searched. The RCMP confiscated 131 forty-ounce bottles of assorted liquors, four twenty-six-ounce bottles, seven and a half gallons of alcohol, and nine cartons of cigarettes.

The vessel was released a few days later upon payment of a $650 fine.

As can be seen, overall quantities in the post-Confederation era throughout the 1970s were relatively small, and the fines were not of an unbearable nature, so they were not deterrents to this historical rumrunning trade.

The *Lacsa* was used to bring ashore in Rhode Island alcohol taken in international waters. Her decks are covered with barrels of pure alcohol.
(Photo courtesy of Mr. James Miller)

Cutter *Alachasse* discharging seized alcohol in Pictou, Nova Scotia.
(Photo courtesy of Captain R. C. Butt)

**Tins of pure white alcohol were in high demand
on the Burin Peninsula contraband trade.**
(Photo courtesy of Mr. Lucien Girardin-Dagort)

Once landed on the Burin Peninsula, liquor shipments were often hidden in the woods prior to being transported to market. (Author collection)

RCMP officers on the Burin Peninsula with seized shipment of alcohol. (Author collection)

Small sheds along deserted stretches of beaches on the Burin Peninsula were used on occasion to hide contraband shipments until they could be transported to market. (Author collection)

A quantity of tobacco and alcohol seized by RCMP in a small shed located along the shoreline of the Burin Peninsula. (Author collection)

RUMRUNNERS KIDNAP AN RCMP OFFICER

The early part of the 1980s was no different than the previous two decades. History kept repeating itself; the typical seizure in early December 1983 was as it had been in the past. An eighteen-foot dory was intercepted by the RCMP patrol vessel *Centennial* two miles off Fortune Head.

Police confiscated fourteen cases of liquor and a two-and-a-half-gallon container of alcohol, hardly a major interception of Christmas cheer. It probably cost taxpayers more in trying to enforce the law than the few dollars of taxes on liquor that was being evaded.

From the mid-1980s onward, drastic changes were to take place. The slow dories were being replaced by fibreglass speedboats equipped with powerful outboard engines. These boats could cross the body of water separating Newfoundland from St. Pierre in a matter of minutes rather than the two or three hours each way required by the slow dories. The rumrunners were going high-tech.

* * *

A rather unusual incident took place in May of 1987. While it was usually Newfoundlanders who made the crossing to St. Pierre to procure contraband, there were exceptions when French fishermen would get involved in the trade.

Two French fishermen were unloading a shipment of liquor and cigarettes in Pie Duck Point near Point May, on the toe of the boot of the Burin Peninsula.

RCMP officers apprehended the two Frenchmen and three residents of Fortune who were receiving the goods on shore. As the St. Pierre residents cut the mooring of their boat in an attempt to escape, one RCMP officer, a member of the federal enforcement section, jumped aboard. His colleague was meanwhile busy arresting the three Newfoundlanders.

While the Mountie was waving his revolver, the French dory was already some metres away from the shore.

The two Frenchmen initially agreed to return to land but convinced the officer that the surf was too high to safely disembark.

They were telling him it was too dangerous in the dark with a small dory and big waves. The rumrunners said it must have made quite a impression on the officer, as he proposed they go to another beach, where they again encountered high waves. They tried the first beach once more, but this time the two rumrunners complained their hands were too sore to continue rowing and asked permission to start the dory's engine.

Suspicious that the rumrunners were about to set sail for French territory, the officer again threatened them with his revolver.

One of the Frenchmen dared the officer. "Go ahead, shoot us."

One of the rumrunners said the officer turned white as a ghost and said, "Sorry, sorry."

"He had to be frightened for sure," commented the rumrunners, since when a policeman asks for your forgiveness he's got to be scared.

One of the rumrunners then pointed out to the officer that they could as easily set off for St. Pierre or Green Island. This was not a threat or an invitation. Both parties had their cards to play, and they played them.

The officer then said, "No, please. Let me off at the beach."

The rumrunners agreed to let the officer off at a beach a few hundred metres from where they were first surprised unloading the liquor. The deal was that they agreed to dump the rest of the contraband overboard. The rumrunners stated that, in return, the officer agreed to let them go free.

They said that the officer then shook hands with them and helped them dispose of the contraband over the side.

They landed him as agreed and set sail for St. Pierre.

On the shoreline, thirty-six cases of liquor, seventy-five litres of alcohol, and fifteen cartons of cigarettes were seized.

The incident resulted in charges of kidnapping being laid against the rumrunners by the RCMP.

The rumrunners countered by stating that they did not kidnap anyone. It seemed that if someone jumped on your boat, it could hardly be called a kidnapping.

It was rather an embarrassing episode for the RCMP. The officer in question refused to tell his story to the press. His supervising sergeant would not comment on the rumrunner's version except to say, "They can say whatever they want, but there's two sides to this story!"

Kidnapping charges were eventually dropped. The two rumrunners were given fines when they went to court in Grand Bank. Of the three Newfoundlanders involved, one, a seventy-three-year-old man, was given a stiffer fine of $1,500, as it was his second conviction for smuggling liquor from the French Islands, while the two other men were given fines of $750 each.

This officially put an end to this bizarre incident. Meanwhile, on the Burin Peninsula, where rumrunning is considered part of their tradition, collective cartoons and special t-shirts relating to the incident stated making their appearance.

* * *

In its annual report for 1987, the Canadian Association of Chiefs of Police stated that smuggling contraband liquor and cigarettes from St. Pierre and Miquelon was an ancient practice that continued to be both widespread and profitable.

Investigators in Newfoundland had made four separate seizures of smuggled liquor and cigarettes during the year, and the contra-band value of the haul, including seized vehicles motors and gear amounted to a mere $13,000.

In spite of the claim that the smuggling was widespread, the police association's organized crime committee was unable to give any estimate of the value or volume of contraband that flowed from the neighbouring French Islands. It would appear that with such a low seizure rate, the rumrunners were able to outmanoeuvre the RCMP, as it was no secret to anyone that St. Pierre liquor was readily available along the shore.

A major change that would favour the rumrunners took place in early April 1988. The RCMP patrol vessel *Centennial*, which had been a common sight in southern coast waters for thirteen years, was officially retired from active duty. The *Centennial* was operated by the RCMP on that part of the coast to curb smuggling.

At a ceremony held to decommission the vessel, the chief super-intendent, commanding officer of B Division, stated that the with-drawal of the *Centennial* didn't mean that smuggling activities between the south coast and St. Pierre and Miquelon would be any easier for would-be entrepreneurs. He stated that the RCMP had undertaken to phase the *Centennial* out of service, after a very careful study, and after they had been assured they could perform the duties with smaller vessels that were faster and more manoeu-vrable, such as the Boston Whaler.

The $150,000 maintenance cost per year had been the major factor that had caused the retirement of the vessel. A replacement vessel would cost several million dollars.

In spite of the RCMP's reasoning, this action can probably be singled out as to why the tradition of supplying the south coast rum-runners liquor and tobacco for Newfoundland was to increase to the point where the trade picked up to levels that resembled a smaller version of Prohibition. Makers of high-performance fibreglass ves-sels had a backlog of orders for residents of the south coast in gen-eral. Outboard engine dealers were selling continuously bigger engines that could cut down the time crossing from the Burin Peninsula to St. Pierre to mere minutes.

Throughout 1989, the rumrunning business was brisk. It was no longer the cod fisherman selling a few bottles to his neighbours, but a major business.

Even though there had been little actual seizures since the *Centennial* had been withdrawn, the RCMP were busily at work. It was basically the calm prior to the storm.

Burin Peninsula convenience stores had been found to stop carrying tobacco products, because the market had virtually disappeared due to much lower prices on smuggled tobacco, which was now smuggled in massive quantities.

The floodgates were now open, and numerous speedboats with high-powered engines entered the trade.

The trade had now blossomed into big business. This could be seen from the size of the odd seizure that was occasionally made by land-based RCMP officers. For example, in August of 1989, a large quantity of contraband goods was found stashed near a beach in the Little Lawn area.

The seizure consisted of fifty-one cases of canned tobacco, one case of cigarettes, as well as three cases of alcoholic beverages. The goods had a total street value of over $30,000.

Things were getting out of hand, after only a few months following the withdrawal of the patrol vessel. Then the RCMP decided to act.

The withdrawal in April 1988 of the RCMP cutter *Centennial* opened the flood-gates to the rumrunning trade from St. Pierre. (Author collection)

A high-speed rumrunner heading for the Burin Peninsula.
(Author collection)

Containers of tobacco from Canada would arrive in St. Pierre and find their way back to Newfoundland on high-speed rumrunning vessels.
(Author collection)

OPERATION BLOWTORCH

On December 5, 1989, about 100 RCMP officers from St. John's to Springdale converged on the top of the Burin Peninsula and started searching homes and making arrests. The raid, which police billed as the "biggest smuggling bust" in Newfoundland history, and probably in Canada in the last forty years, carried the code name of "Operation Blowtorch."

A total of seventy-four Newfoundlanders and seven residents of St. Pierre were rounded up. Eleven of the Newfoundlanders, reported to be from the St. John's area, were charged with smuggling offences, in a showdown that was six months in the planning.

The charges laid were conspiracy to smuggle and to evade taxes on smuggled goods, conspiracy to possess goods illegally imported into Canada, and other possession charges under the customs act.

In spite of all of these declarations, the supposed biggest haul in Newfoundland history only netted the RCMP 1,370 forty-ounce bottles of liquor, 354 tubs of tobacco, fifty-two cartons of cigarettes, and 108 one-gallon jugs of pure alcohol, for a total street value of $50,000. As well, police confiscated $100,000 worth of equipment, including boats, motors, and vehicles alleged to have been used in the smuggling operations.

The raid could probably have been much more successful if it had not been for a rumoured indiscretion. It was said that an RCMP's wife from Central Newfoundland, when asked by a neighbour as to the whereabouts of her husband, said that he was on his way to a big raid on the Burin Peninsula. The neighbour, having relatives down the peninsula, quickly tipped off her family, who in turn were able to notify a certain number of other parties from the area. In the next few hours, a lot of contraband was jettisoned, but some of the others were not quite as lucky and were caught and charged.

The superintendent in charge of Operation Blowtorch stated that police seizures had gone from multiple bottles to multiple cases in the few previous months, which although not mentioned, corresponded to the time that the *Centennial* had been withdrawn from patrol duties.

The police veteran wouldn't speculate whether the major bust would result in a decrease of smuggled goods. He said that on a good day, smugglers could transport between 500 to 1,000 cases of liquor from St. Pierre to Newfoundland. The amount being smuggled would result in a loss of millions of dollars in taxes to the provincial and federal governments. Based on this estimate of activity over this short period of time, it is quite apparent millions in taxes had been lost in that time.

When the case made its way to court in Grand Bank, some of the accused chose to be tried by judge and jury. Others pleaded guilty.

Jury trials for this type of incident were unheard of on the Burin Peninsula. In fact, jury selection was blamed for hurting Grand Bank businesses.

The Grand Bank Business Association expressed its concerns to the provincial Minister of Justice. It protested the process followed by the courts in selecting jurors for the trials held at the Grand Bank courthouse in connection with the Operation Blowtorch trials.

The sheriff's office was selecting jurors from Grand Bank, Fortune, and Grand Beach only. They felt that this area comprised a small portion of the Burin Peninsula and placed an exceptional and unfair burden on the individuals and businesses of their communities.

Apparently the cost of drawing jurors from towns outside of this restricted area was the motivating factor for drawing on individuals closer at hand. While appreciating and acknowledging the concerns for costs, the Business Association felt that it should be done on a more equitable basis.

Since businesses were responsible to pay the employee's wages and benefits while serving on jury duty, the association felt that it was rather ironic that law-abiding individuals and business owners had to bear such costs to provide trials for alleged lawbreakers.

In handing down sentences, one of the judges said evidence provided during the trial made it clear that some of the accused were involved in a well-planned, ongoing business that was set up long before police began Operation Blowtorch. It was obvious the accused were in direct competition with the Newfoundland Liquor Corporation and that the amount of alcohol being illegally imported into Canada from the French Islands of St. Pierre and Miquelon was significant. "It was not a victimless crime." He pointed out that the taxpayers of Newfoundland and Canada were all victims.

On a more sinister side, the judge said that regulations to prevent young people from gaining access to alcoholic beverages were being circumvented.

Evidence presented by the Crown during the trial revealed the accused smuggled contraband goods into Newfoundland, mostly alcohol and tobacco products, without detection by police, then placed them in secondary storage, cabins, uninhabited houses, etc., and from there distributed the contraband at a wholesale level and then on to retail customers.

Arrangements were made in St. Pierre with suppliers to acquire the goods which were then surreptitiously brought into Newfoundland.

This was more than a conspiracy; it was a business plan. The accused knew what they were doing; it was a deliberate crime.

Evidence during the trial revealed that trips were made when weather permitted. On some occasions, there were fifteen Newfoundland boats smuggling contraband at the same time. The judge said that this would indicate as much as 1,000 cases of liquor being brought across, in just one day, resulting in a loss of many thousands of dollars to Newfoundland and Canadian Government revenue.

In the case of six of the accused, the judge pointed out that even though they had previous records, involving customs charges, he would not take that into account when considering the penalty. However, he did take into account the attitude of the accused; he stated that, when caught, they would press on. It was a joint venture. All would contribute to any fines or losses through the seizure of any contraband; their intent was to handle their fines through further rumrunning.

A message had to be sent to the community that this type of activity should not be allowed to flourish as an illegal business. However, that message could not be sent through the imposition of fines.

For those convicted, overall sentences in Operation Blowtorch ranged from $1,000 up to $25,000 and from two weeks in jail up to seven months.

The five St. Pierre residents charged in the conspiracy to smuggle goods in Canada eventually surrendered in Newfoundland and appeared in court.

The RCMP alleged that the five were responsible for providing Newfoundland-based smugglers with alcohol and tobacco products for resale in Canada without paying duty or taxes.

They were all released on $15,000 bail per person and ordered to refrain from contact with alleged co-conspirators in Newfoundland.

In the St. Pierre merchants' opinion, they had done nothing wrong. Selling liquor to whoever wanted to buy it was not an illegal practice, and they couldn't understand why they were being dragged in front of Canadian courts, which they felt had no jurisdiction over legal sales that were made in a foreign country.

All charges were eventually dismissed, as there was insufficient evidence to convict them.

Even though residents of the Burin Peninsula were quite upset during Operation Blowtorch, and complained about the police being heavy-handed in house searches, it didn't stop them from replenishing the supplies for the Christmas trade. Only two days after Operation Blowtorch, police seized another 100 one-gallon containers of alcohol in Lamaline.

Operation Blowtorch had demonstrated to the police that the arrests and seizures were only a drop in the bucket compared to the real smuggling activity. They realized that, traditionally, Newfoundlanders hopped in their fishing boats, went to St. Pierre, and returned home with thousands of dollars of alcohol and tobacco. A police spokesman commented that in the same way Newfoundlanders had also traditionally considered poaching of wildlife a natural right, they also considered smuggling liquor a God-given right.

The RCMP spokesman said it was easy to understand how a person would prefer paying one-third less for a bottled of smuggled liquor than paying the official retail price. This widespread acceptance of the practice made information difficult, if not impossible, to find out the true extent and cost of the smuggling activities. Enforcement of contraband regulations was very difficult, unless police were tipped to a specific incident. It was a rare occurrence for them to make a seizure.

After the magnitude of Operation Blowtorch revelations, the police spokesman had to admit that the withdrawal of the RCMP cutter *Centennial* had made the body of water between St. Pierre and Newfoundland all but open territory.

In spite of the Boston Whaler being available, it wasn't very useful in winter weather. He concluded his statement with the fact that, "It's pretty difficult to nip it in the bud, since leaving St. Pierre, you've got nothing to go after it with."

This showed that the illusions of a few months earlier, when the *Centennial* had been retired, had been miscalculated. The next few months, the wide-open straits would register a traffic of rumrunners like it had never seen since the days of Prohibition in the '20s and '30s.

* * *

History on the Burin Peninsula was being written as the court cases for twenty-five accused in Operation Blowtorch, of various offences under the Criminal Code of Canada and the Canada Customs Act, came to a conclusion.

Eleven people pleaded guilty to charges of conspiracy to smuggle goods into Canada and conspiracy to evade taxes. Others pleaded not guilty and elected trial by judge and jury. The trial took nine weeks.

There were eight women and four men on the jury. Much of the testimony they heard was of a very technical nature, dealing with undercover activities, detailing the operations of the wiretap surveillance officers of the RCMP during the five months of the investigation, which had taken place in the summer and fall of 1989.

The report-a-smuggler program enacted earlier in the year, whereby citizens could report smuggling activities and obtain as a reward a percentage of the value, seemed to have had some attraction. One such phone call to the St. Lawrence RCMP detachment led them to a stash of liquor, alcohol, and tobacco products hidden behind some rocks at the entrance of Lawn Harbour.

RCMP sources were claiming that the Burin Peninsula smuggling operations were now highly commercialized, resulting in the loss of hundreds of thousands of dollars in revenues to both the Newfoundland and federal governments annually.

An old house on the Burin Peninsula which was raided during Operation Blowtorch – a large cache of contraband alcohol was found. The boat in front was used to transport liquor from St. Pierre; it was seized by RCMP. (Author collection)

A large cache of bagged cases of alcohol seized in a house during Operation Blowtorch. (Author collection)

An RCMP van hauls away a quantity of cases of alcohol seized in an old house during Operation Blowtorch. (Author collection)

Old cars of little value would be used to transport the contraband from the Burin Peninsula all over the island. (Author collection)

Some of the boats seized by RCMP during Operation Blowtorch.
(Author collection)

**RCMP evidence room where seized items were tagged
before cases went to trial.**
(Author collection)

Seized sixty-ounce bottles of Canadian distilled whisky bottled in the U.S. sent to St. Pierre and on to Newfoundland. (Author collection)

Small containers of pure alcohol seized in an RCMP raid on Burin Peninsula. (Author collection)

Inauguration of the RCMP high-speed catamaran *Simmonds*. It was a contributing factor in curbing the contraband market that operated between St. Pierre and the Burin Peninsula in the late 1980s and 1990s. (Author collection)

The RCMP patrol vessel *Simmonds* is said to attain speeds of thirty-eight knots.
(Author collection)

SMUGGLING IN 1991

During 1991, smuggling operations continued on a large scale; the RCMP were mostly ineffective at curbing the activities. The rumrunners were so well-organized that the handful of RCMP officers and the means that were available to them could hardly put a dent in the flourishing traffic. There were more arrests in 1991, but they represented a small percentage of the trafficking compared to the volume that made its way to market.

In the second part of June, 4,000 tubs of tobacco were seized from a house in Point May, along with a few bottles of alcohol and twenty cartons of cigarettes. The street value of the seizure was about $14,000. A twenty-seven-year-old Point May man was arrested. Later in the month, two twenty-two-year-old St. Lawrence men were arrested on the Burin Peninsula highway while making a routine delivery of twenty-eight cases of assorted liquor. The retail value of the goods seized was about $10,000.

For a certain period, liquor was carried to market by older cars. In case of arrest, these cars would be confiscated by the Crown but were really of little value. The RCMP were more likely to stop older vehicles in their routine checks, as there was a likelihood that these were carrying smuggled liquor. The young men driving these vehicles were usually just hired by the rumrunners to make the delivery trip. In case of interception and arrest by the RCMP, the owner of the smuggled merchandise would usually secretly arrange to pay the fines for those found guilty and sentenced to pay.

In August 1991, a twenty-six-year-old Point May resident was charged with possession of forty-four cartons of cigarettes, twelve bottles of liquor, and eleven jugs of pure white alcohol, locally known as Alky. Within the next few days, three more arrests would take place. A twenty-four-year-old Lamaline resident was arrested with forty-four jugs of alcohol, sixty bottles of liquor, and twenty cartons of cigarettes. Later that month, a thirty-four-year-old resident of Lawn was arrested in the Marystown area with contraband goods, consisting of eleven cases of liquor, and fifty cartons of cigarettes valued at more than $5,000. The following day a Marystown resident was arrested, having in his possession nine cases of liquor, sixty cartons of cigarettes, and seven jugs of alcohol.

The following month a twenty-three-year-old Grand Bank resident led undercover RCMP officers to a home on Empire Avenue in St. John's, where they found a stash of tobacco.

RCMP seized 264 tins of tobacco with a value of $10,500. In addition to seizing $2,510 in cash, the smuggler had been under surveillance for some time. The same month, it was the turn of a thirty-year-old Marystown man to be arrested following a so-called routine check. The RCMP discovered fifty-nine cases of assorted liquor, mostly whisky and rum in sixty-ounce bottles, with a total street value of $16,000.

In 1991, there was a tremendous increase in smuggled tobacco to Newfoundland; this was loose tobacco for roll-your-own cigarettes. This was due to the delivery of new federal and provincial budgets which imposed big tobacco hikes. This in turn created an increased demand for the much cheaper smuggled tobacco, and thus savings for consumers and big profits for the smugglers.

In October 1991, a thirty-seven-year-old woman and twenty-eight-year-old man from St. John's were arrested on the highway between Grand Bank and Marystown, in a nine-year-old car that was loaded with $9,000 worth of liquor, tobacco, and alcohol.

In November there was another spectacular operation code-named "Operation Bucket." It involved a four-month investigation aimed at curbing smuggling operations on the Burin Peninsula. It was similar in strategy to the 1989 "Operation Blowtorch," except that it was on a smaller scale. In this case, thirty RCMP officers from the Burin Peninsula and a member of the general investigation section took part in this operation, which resulted in the seizure of a quantity of tobacco and alcohol.

Tobacco-laden car seized by RCMP on the Burin highway. (Author collection)

Twelve men from the Point May and Fortune areas were arrested. The RCMP confiscated a number of vehicles at the same time.

Later in the month of November, RCMP on the Burin Peninsula continued their attempt to crack down on the ever-flourishing smuggling operation from the French Islands of St. Pierre and Miquelon.

The combined forces of the RCMP from Gander, Marystown, and Grand Bank descended upon the English Harbour East communities, where they seized eighty cases of assorted liquor in sixty-ounce bottles that were stashed in an area near the community. The liquor consisted of mostly whisky and rum, and had a street value of close to $22,000. No arrests were made.

About the same time, the Marystown RCMP detachment seized a vehicle and confiscated fifty cartons of cigarettes and sixty tubs of tobacco. A thirty-nine-year-old Lawn resident was subsequently arrested. The value of the seizure was reported to be in the vicinity of $5,000.

Just before Christmas 1991, a thirty-eight-year-old Point May rumrunner lost his life. A gasoline can and an oar was all that was discovered on the Grand Bank shoreline following the tragedy. It was identified as belonging to the borrowed boat in which the Point May resident had gone missing on the late afternoon of December 19. The RCMP in Grand Bank were notified early the next morning that the man had not returned as scheduled. It was diplomatically explained as an accident while the man was out bird hunting.

The eighteen-foot fibreglass boat had sailed in late afternoon with contraband from St. Pierre in heavy weather and was lost. No one will ever know how the blue-hulled vessel bearing the familiar name *Blowtorch One* went down. She could have been swamped by a wave or hit a partially submerged object at high speed.

The *Blowtorch One* was owned by a Lamaline man who had been convicted of smuggling and sentenced to five months in jail as a result of Operation Blowtorch.

While serving his sentence in the Clarenville Correctional Centre, he refurbished his boat and fibreglassed the hull while on day parole for employment training purposes.

A coastline search by aircraft helicopters and several vessels had failed to find a trace of the boat or its lone occupant.

Storm-force winds, gusting to thirty knots, freezing temperatures, and snow squalls had hit the Burin Peninsula during the afternoon and evening of December 19, causing rough seas on the return trip, which caused this fatality. Such incidents causing the death of a rumrunner were very unusual, especially considering the number that was said to venture between St. Pierre and the Newfoundland coast.

The year had ended with numerous convictions, which were getting substantially higher. Many had been sentenced to jail terms and heavy fines in Operation Blowtorch, which was now winding down. Fines were now up to the $5,000 level, unheard of in previous years.

Judges involved in hearing these cases had a certain degree of satisfaction. According to Provincial Court Judge G. Handrigan, it was commonly believed that offences under revenue statutes such as the income tax act, retail sales tax, and customs act were victimless crimes, by which it was believed that no real harm resulted to the public, only a loss to the treasuries of the government.

In his summation in a case involving liquor smuggling charges against a man-and-wife team from Swift Current, he stated, "All members of the public suffer by reason of such offences, because of the diminishment of the resource base and a drain on the resources of our governments to meet the huge expenditures of their departments."

In summation of a case involving a man from Marystown who was convicted by a jury for evasion of taxes and possession of contraband unlawfully imported into Canada, Supreme Court Justice Gordon Easton stated that a conviction by a Burin Peninsula jury dispelled certain myths. "Your conviction by a jury is significant. I have heard and I am sure it is an open secret that the bet was that juries on the Burin Peninsula would not convict on smuggling or related offences. That myth has now been put to rest."

Judge Easton went on to say that he thought the accused was, in essence, "a product of history and a casualty of geography." He went on to say that, in the 1920s and 1930s, St. Pierre was a haven for rumrunners and coincidentally a comfort for Newfoundlanders in the years of depression.

"No one really considered smuggling as a crime in those days," he said. "Given the poverty of the time and the needs of Newfoundlanders for something to relieve the nagging misery of their existence, that feeling was probably understandable."

Songs and stories praising the exploits of the rumrunners are common in the folklore of our province. However, Judge Easton said the mystique of their stories is grudgingly dying.

According to him, in the 1990s, smuggling had not only become an economic burden, but more importantly a social problem. The proportions of the illegality had taken away from the thrill and mystique and the criminality of the smuggling, and its magnitude was now first and foremost a major concern.

On the other hand, the two police stings, Operation Blowtorch, 1989, and Operation Bucket, 1991, were the first times that police had wiretapped phones to catch smugglers.

* * *

Operation Blowtorch had brought everything into the open. People were really paranoid. Now they were using codes on the phones, asking for fish or paint or other items as a substitute for what they really meant: booze.

As time passed in Point May, where smugglers painted their boats a dark colour to blend into the night or the fog, residents made no show of wealth that would tip police to their activities. Still, phones were being tapped.

One resident complained, "It's desperate. You're paying for your phone and you can't use it. There's no privacy at all. The police are doing whatever they want around here; they are turning residents against each other."

One resident claimed that he had been rumrunning most of his life and that his father and grandfather before him. He had no intentions of voluntarily stopping it, and he in fact intended to help his neighbours get the job done. "There's honour among thieves. We loan each other motors if need be."

Unique way of transporting contraband in old vehicle on the Burin highway.
(Author collection)

Seized twenty-two-foot rumrunning craft that operated with liquor and tobacco shipments between St. Pierre and Burin Peninsula. (Author collection)

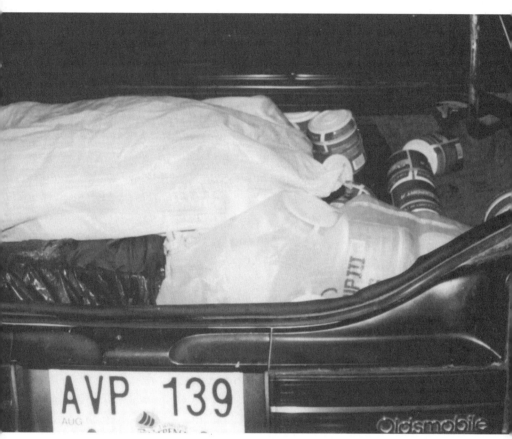

Seized car transporting shipment of tobacco on Burin highway.
(Author collection)

SMUGGLING IN 1992

The second day of 1992 saw the first contraband seizures on the Burin Peninsula, where the RCMP Grand Bank detachment seized $10,000 worth of liquor and tobacco near the Point May area. As was often the case, it was stashed away without any arrests being made.

This first week of January also saw the preliminary hearings for "Operation Bucket," the latest of police operations resulting in the arrests of five men and five women from the Burin Peninsula on ten charges, following an RCMP investigation which took place from September 1 to November 5.

By mid-January 1992, due to the magnitude of smuggling caused by the withdrawal of the patrol vessel *Centennial* four years earlier, RCMP decided to reintroduce a patrol vessel.

P. D. Carven, superintendent and officer in charge of the criminal operation branch of the RCMP, announced that they were immediately deploying the *Fort McCloud,* a forty-three-foot patrol vessel, for duties along the south coast.

The *McCloud* was to be complemented at sea by a Boston Whaler, and fast-rescue craft, which currently patrolled the area. Patrols were to be coordinated with land, sea, and air surveillance personnel. The police superintendent stated that equipment and off-load sites would be monitored regularly. He also stated that it was the beginning of increased marine vigilance and that additional resources would be deployed as required to repress smuggling. The

Fort McCloud was to perform duties similar to those of the *Centennial* that had been withdrawn from service because of the exorbitant cost of maintaining that type of surveillance. Police were now admitting that enforcement methods of the previous four years had met with limited success.

It was now estimated that smuggling activities from St. Pierre represented an annual loss in federal and provincial tax revenue of $15,000,000 – $20,000,000. It was furthermore stated that the smuggling of tobacco and liquor products into Newfoundland from St. Pierre was increasing at an alarming rate.

From the police point of view, smuggling was having an adverse effect on local communities, through incidents of youths consuming poisonous liquids, alcohol abuse, and life-threatening incidents encountered while transporting contraband in small open boats.

Everyone realized that the high taxes that were being imposed by both federal and provincial governments on liquor and tobacco products made smuggling a very viable business.

Smugglers using the small open boats, equipped with two very powerful outboard engines, made very good profits from goods purchases with substantially less taxes in St. Pierre, and reselling at bargain prices compared to the ones charged to consumers by Newfoundland Government liquor stores on tobacco retailers.

Smuggling was really a way of life on the peninsula. A trouble-free trip to St. Pierre could earn the rumrunner $3,000 when the cargo was sold in Newfoundland.

One rumrunner commented that he liked the excitement of evading police who patrolled the foggy shores of the peninsula, as he waited for the flicker of flashing lights that signalled to him that all was clear to land. He said, "It's in the blood. It gets your adrenaline going. The scary part is who's going to be waiting for you, your boys or the police, but I don't panic over it. If I get caught, I get caught."

Along the tip of the Burin Peninsula, smuggling goods from St. Pierre, a mere twelve miles away or twenty-minute boat ride by the high-powered vessels used by rumrunners, was traditionally viewed as a harmless perk, a right of existence.

What was traditionally a way to save money on liquor and cigarettes had mushroomed into a multi-million dollar business in the last three or four years.

RCMP *Fort McCloud* off Green Island, NL, trying to find rumrunners.
(Author collection)

Police stated that the recession, a disastrous fishery, and the federal GST had all had a hand in pushing smuggling to new heights. According to Corporal Derrick Anthony, the province's RCMP Customs and Excise coordinator at the time in St. John's, "It's now become a very intricate network of distribution. We're dealing with a form of organized crime." He stated that it wasn't hard for smugglers to find others sympathetic to their activities.

Police realized things had gotten worse three or four years earlier, when retail sales of liquor and cigarettes plummeted on the

Burin Peninsula. It was the first clue that smugglers were hiding more and more contraband in the fir-lined hills along Smuggler's Road, a bumpy gravel path outside Fortune that skirts the shoreline, or burying the goods in bogs where police dogs couldn't sniff them out.

A local resident of the Burin Peninsula commented that smugglers were a distinct society. They figured they had a right to it. "Well, there's nothing to work at in the area: fishing and smuggling, that's it."

New boats with powerful engines began showing up near the bright clapboard houses in towns along the southern tip of the Burin Peninsula. Some of these houses had a picture-perfect view of the smuggling paradise of St. Pierre.

Unexpected news arrived in mid-February when federal Revenue Minister Otto Jelinek announced an export tax on Canadian cigarettes and tobacco products, as well as higher fines and jail terms for smugglers. An export tax of $8.00 would be applied for cigarettes, and $5.33 per tin of tobacco. In all products sold for export, this was expected to have a significant impact on the smuggling trade on the south coast of Newfoundland as well as other parts of Canada, when tobacco smuggling was becoming a major problem.

Legislation was also being proposed to raise the maximum fine for smuggling from $50,000 to $200,000.

The threat of heavier fines didn't deter would-be smugglers, as a large stash of tobacco and alcohol valued at $35,000 was discovered by police near Little St. Lawrence in late March 1992, but police were unable to track down the owners.

Meanwhile, the tobacco lobby was hard at work trying to get the government to reverse its export tax on their tobacco products. They made no secret that they would transfer their production of export products to the United States to avoid the taxes and remain in business.

Apparently, a coalition of seven groups, including tobacco growers unions, retailers, and distributors was also hard at work to have the taxes rolled back. They were successful, as the federal government was compelled to remove the short-lived export tax by April.

The revenue minister diplomatically admitted that there was a smuggling problem, but that government and the tobacco industry agreed upon the removal of the tax, and to work on ways to cut smuggling. The industry agreed to develop new packaging and markings to differentiate between export and domestic tobacco products.

Several seizures were made in the first half of 1992, among which involved a twenty-two-year-old from St. Lawrence. His car went out of control and flipped over when being chased by the RCMP near Lord's Cove on the Burin Peninsula. After the crash, the occupant was taken to hospital, where he was treated for minor injuries. Police confiscated from the car 200 tins of tobacco, and a dozen sixty-ounce bottles of liquor valued at $8,500.

Strangely enough, the same person had been arrested on the Burin Peninsula eleven days previously by the Marystown RCMP, having in his possession 120 bottles of liquor valued at $4,800.

The RCMP were on their part strongly satisfied with the significant increase in the number of charges laid against smugglers during the first six months of the year.

So far, in 1992, thirteen people had been charged with customs and excise violations, compared to four charged during the same period the previous year.

The RCMP stated that the total value of tobacco seized so far that year was $30,000.

They attributed the increase to several factors, such as more awareness by the general public, the report-a-smuggler program, and the use of confidential sources, as well as increased surveillance by the police force on the Burin Peninsula.

The total value of all contraband seized by the combined forces of the Burin Peninsula detachments amounted to over $100,000.

In late June 1992, a forty-eight-year-old resident of Paradise was arrested near St. Lawrence as he was transporting 216 sixty-ounce bottles of contraband liquor, valued at about $10,000.

Yet another attempt to curb smuggling was initiated by the government in July 1992. Canadian distillers had a quota on the amount of liquor being sold to St. Pierre. By the end of the month, the quota had been reached. This measure had, in fact, little effect. The St. Pierre distributors who supplied the Newfoundland rumrunners now purchased additional supplies of Canadian whisky sent in bulk from Canada and bottled by U.S. bottlers under little-known brand names. The rum was U.S. Virgin Island, which was not the same quality as Canadian distilled products, but that was all that was available, so it had to do, since additional Canadian-brand goods would not be available until a new quota was made available the following year. The U.S.-bottled goods had one advantage: they were cheaper.

The fact that it was different liquor than what they had been used to didn't deter the rumrunners. In September, a thirty-one-year-old man from Chapel Arm, Trinity Bay, was arrested with more than 300 bottles of contraband liquor, close to the junction of the Burin Peninsula and the Trans-Canada Highway.

Another unusual case was the sentencing of a senior citizen to a fine of $1,000. The sixty-six-year-old Lamaline woman had been charged with possession of contraband as a result of Operation Bucket some months earlier.

Police had only seized a small quantity in a raid on her house but introduced interceptions of private communications as evidence in the case.

In passing sentence, Judge G. Handrigan stated that he had to take into consideration the significance of deterrence. "The whole idea is to get a message across to the public that this is not acceptable behaviour. The cavalier attitude of the public toward smuggling, the fines, and the manner in which the public goes about finding ways around the system is very disconcerting."

In yet another incident, a fifty-eight-year-old Point May man was fined $2,500 after pleading guilty to two charges of possession of contraband goods, as well as possession of tobacco not properly stamped. The sentencing followed the seizure of thirty-eight cartons of cigarettes, 138 tins of tobacco, and a quantity of liquor having a total value of $8,000.

As was the traditional custom for decades, there was an increased demand for the Christmas season. The RCMP were also stepping up surveillance, and the net result was a series of big seizures. The combined forces of the St. Lawrence detachment and members of the St. John's subdivision of the Customs and Excise branch confiscated liquor and tobacco products with a street value of more than $20,000. In three separate raids, fifty cases of assorted liquor and five cases of tobacco were confiscated. A fifty-five-year-old Lawn man, a forty-five-year-old St. Lawrence resident, and a twenty-two-year-old St. John's man were arrested as a result.

The Grand Bank detachment intercepted a vehicle near Come by Chance, where they found 120 sixty-ounce bottles of liquor.

A few days prior to Christmas, members of the Corner Brook federal enforcement section, assisted by provincial wildlife officials and the Burgeo RCMP, seized alcohol and tobacco products with a street value of $16,500. They also seized a twenty-foot boat and two outboard motors, along with other equipment. In this particular case, the contraband goods were believed to have been imported from Miquelon, which is located closer to the southwest coast than St. Pierre.

The last big seizure of the year occurred just before Christmas 1992, when a quantity of tobacco was seized from a vehicle on Route 210 near Terrenceville. A male resident of Lawn was arrested in this particular case; the tobacco had a street value of $20,000.

Analyzing the year that had gone by, Corporal Derrick Anthony, provincial Customs and Excise coordinator, stated that seizures of contraband goods originating from the French Islands of St. Pierre and Miquelon had almost doubled in the past year.

Corporal Anthony stated that current economic conditions may have been the reason why more people were taking part in this illegal activity. It was so lucrative and the economy was so bad that people do it. Some people did who were not so inclined two years earlier. Some people were making huge profits and smuggling contraband goods in a way to make a quick dollar. It was profitable enough for some people to take the risks.

Since smuggling had increased dramatically, it was inevitable that the numbers of people being charged would also increase. From 1991 to 1992, the number of charges laid nearly doubled. In 1991, 180 persons were charged under the customs act, whereas in 1992, the number rose to 312.

The reason for the increase of charges was an increase in tobacco smuggling. Tobacco was more easily concealed than liquor and easier to get rid of. Corporal Anthony stated that it was no surprise that the smuggling of tobacco products had increased in 1992, as it was considered the preferred commodity among smugglers, due to increasing taxes being placed on Canadian tobacco.

Illegal, loose tobacco could be purchased from the smugglers at less than half the price of duty-paid tobacco in retail stores.

Corporal Anthony said that for those caught illegally smuggling liquor or tobacco into Newfoundland, fines could range up to several thousands of dollars, and include jail terms, depending on the amount seized. Culprits could be required to pay duty taxes on the goods confiscated, and their boats were subject to confiscation.

Corporal Anthony also stated that his department had used every method of interception available to fight smuggling in the province, and was willing to try anything to stop it. In spite of the report-a-smuggler program that was in effect, it still didn't stop the flow of tobacco and alcohol to Newfoundland.

Suitcases would at times be used to transport tobacco on local taxi service to St. John's. (Author collection)

Bags of contraband alcohol seized in one of the numerous RCMP raids on the Burin Peninsula. (Author collection)

SMUGGLING IN 1993

The new year, 1993, didn't bring a slowdown in smuggling activities, as in early January, three men from the Burin Peninsula community of Epworth were arrested in connection with alleged smuggling of alcohol and tobacco.

Considerable ingenuity had been used to hide the contraband goods. Some were hidden in an underground room in one suspect's home, while more was recovered from a space behind a secret wall panel in another residence.

The RCMP stated that the value of the contraband was in excess of $20,000.

The statistics on smuggling activities in the Burin Peninsula region dictated the need for increased federal enforcement in 1993.

The police admitted that they had no firm or accurate account of the actual amount of goods being smuggled into Newfoundland from St. Pierre, but suggested that it could run into the millions of dollars in lost revenues to both the provincial and federal treasuries.

As a result it was decided to open up facilities in Burin, known as the Customs and Excise Section of the RCMP, which would be manned by six members.

The new federal section was to work in close liaison with the three Burin Peninsula detachments, as well as detachment members in Clarenville, Whitbourne, and St. John's. The police felt that being based in Burin also enabled the Customs and Excise Section to patrol the Burin Peninsula more efficiently. The main Burin highway was the only road link to other sections of the province, and was considered the main artery for the transport and distribution of smuggled tobacco and liquor products.

Some rumrunners reacted to these new police measures by adding additional fuel capacity to their fast boats, and delivering their contraband to some St. Mary's Bay location. This would avoid possible interception in the Burin Peninsula highway corridor.

In February 1993, seven people were convicted on charges of possession of goods illegally imported from St. Pierre. The total value of goods seized, which included cigarettes, loose tobacco, and assorted liquor, amounted to $45,000. The maximum fine was $4,000 against a St. Lawrence man who had been arrested near Swift Current with $18,000 worth of tobacco products in his vehicle.

The commanding officer of the new Customs and Excise Section commented that it was big business, and that with the additional manpower, it was hoped the law could more forcefully curb the smuggling activities.

Meanwhile, it was announced that general policing services by the RCMP were to be reduced, but the provincial finance minister sent out a warning to smugglers in his March 1993 budget.

He stated that the RCMP would have $600,000 cut from their general policing services, but in a specialized area, $210,000 had been supplied to employ additional officers to provide a deterrent against smuggling.

The finance minister stated that the government was losing enormous amounts of money through the smuggling of tobacco and alcohol products. Penalties would be increased for those convicted of smuggling offences, and there would be a permanent suspension of licences for any person or business found selling or buying smuggled goods.

In spite of these new policings and warnings, the flow of liquor and tobacco products continued. In early April, the RCMP seized $35,000 worth of contraband goods in three separate raids. The biggest portion of this was found in two vehicles, northbound on the

Burin Peninsula highway near Mooring Cove, carrying a total of twenty-two cases of contraband tobacco.

Every imaginative way was used to bring the contraband goods to market. In one instance in late April 1993, police stopped a Burin Peninsula taxi that was heading for St. John's. The minivan with nine passengers on board was stopped outside of Marystown. A search of the luggage compartment revealed ninety 1.75-litre bottles of liquor and ten five-litre jugs of pure white alcohol.

A twenty-four-year-old Lamaline man who was a passenger on the bus claimed ownership of the goods that had been stashed in hockey bags, overnight bags, and suitcases.

There were several other incidents involving courier cars that were intercepted on the highway.

In the third week of May 1993, the RCMP reported that they had seized more than $100,000 worth of tobacco and alcohol products thus far during the month.

It was stated that stepped-up federal enforcement by the RCMP Customs and Excise Section was paying big dividends in the number of customs seizures. The RCMP claimed that this did not reflect an increase in smuggling activity, but was more a reflection of new initiatives that were now in place to detect infractions of the customs and excise acts.

With increased manpower and better surveillance, they were better able to put the magnitude of this problem into perspective.

The latest seizure was four unattended vehicles found in a parking lot of a Marystown motel. There was a total of 1,526 200-gram tubs of tobacco with a street value of about $65,000. The vehicle owners, three from St. Lawrence and the other from Marystown, were taken into custody for questioning.

There was a rash of seizures all over the peninsula. The RCMP were now claiming that the amount of contraband being brought into the Burin Peninsula had become alarming, and that it was being transported through other sections of the province by whatever means possible.

RCMP officials stated that high unemployment and the

prospects of quick money appeared to have been luring more and more young people into these smuggling activities.

In June 1993, the RCMP apprehended, at sea, a forty-five-foot longliner transporting contraband goods which consisted of 1,000 litres of liquor, 250 litres of pure alcohol, 150 tubs of tobacco, and ten cartons of cigarettes. The goods were apparently destined for distribution in the south coast communities of Burgeo and Ramea. Two men from Burgeo were arrested to face charges under the customs act.

During the same month, the provincial finance minister fired warning shots across the bows of the rumrunners and their associates. As promised in his March budget, he announced plans in the House of Assembly whereby the provincial government would amend the liquor control act to increase fines for smugglers from $1,000 to $50,000, and implement provisions which would see any business selling smuggled products lose its vending licence.

The finance minister said that stiffener penalties were needed to help stem the tide of smuggled products entering the province, which may cost the provincial treasury from $10,000,000 – $20,000,000 annually. It was felt that it had a serious impact on revenues.

In spite of this, it would be a while before these new fines would be levied by the courts, and meanwhile it was business as usual for the rumrunners. In the third week of July 1993, two separate sweeps by RCMP units on the Burin Peninsula netted more than $40,000 worth of contraband liquor and tobacco.

The RCMP reported that a half-ton pickup truck was stopped on the highway. Upon examination it was found to be carrying 449 tins of smuggled tobacco with an estimated street value of $20,000. The vehicle had been modified to help conceal the goods.

In another seizure on the night of September 23, 1993, RCMP gave chase to a suspected rumrunner, a twenty-three-year-old man from St. John's who was formerly from St. Lawrence. He escaped and made a diversion off the main highway into the community of Parker's Cove, where he abandoned his vehicle and fled into the woods on foot.

The police seized the vehicle, which they found filled with contraband consisting of 336 1.75-litre bottles of liquor, with a street value of $16,000, and 120 tubs of tobacco with a street value of $5,000.

The RCMP later arrested him on the main highway, and he was sentenced to three months in jail, plus a fine of $3,900, or in default of payment, another three months in jail. This was another stiff sentence.

In September 1993, three Lawn residents netted stiff fines relating to contraband charges. One was fined $22,500 or one year in jail, a second received a fine of $10,500 or nine months in jail, and the third $9,500 or eight months in jail.

The stiffer fines were the result of recent changes in the excise act in effect since June 10, 1993. As of then, anyone charged under the act was made to face minimum fines of double the amount of excise tax evaded. The maximum fine was set at triple the amount of tax evaded.

For the first time ever, in September 1993, there was violence between rumrunners and the RCMP.

Two plainclothes officers were searching a vehicle for contraband. They had been unable to locate the car's owner, and while a search warrant was being prepared, a crowd of about 100 St. Lawrence residents surrounded the two RCMP officers and assaulted them. Subsequently, three brothers from St. Lawrence were arrested and charged with assault, obstruction, and mischief causing damage.

The vehicle, a 1984 Ford LTD, was later searched and revealed the presence of 102 1.75-litre bottles of contraband in the trunk.

Two days later, RCMP in St. Lawrence seized 428 1.75-litre bottles of liquor, five cases of tobacco, and 109 cartons of cigarettes, with a street value of $30,000. Police also seized a van. No arrests were made, though the suspects were in the process of unloading the van when the raid was made. The suspects fled on foot into the woods before being apprehended.

At the annual review of organized crime in the country in

September 1993, the Canadian Association of Police Chiefs reported that one of Atlantic Canada's oldest businesses, the contraband trade between Newfoundland and St. Pierre, was booming once again. They reported an increase in the decades-old illicit trade in tobacco and alcohol from St. Pierre, the historical smuggler's haven.

The chiefs of police believed federal and provincial tax hikes on tobacco and alcohol products to be largely responsible for the increasing trade, boosting the profits for smugglers. It was stated to be a lucrative business where one could more than double one's money. A 200-gram tin of tobacco that could be purchased in St. Pierre for $5.00 would be sold in Newfoundland for $23.00. At the same time, a store with tobacco having all of its taxes paid would sell identical products for up to twice that price. It is little wonder that there was a strong demand for contraband tobacco products.

At the same meeting, it was revealed by police that they had begun to act on new federal laws that allowed for the seizure of any proceeds from crime.

As a result of this and the new, hefty fines, 1993 was to be a pivotal year, when rumrunning would suddenly witness a notable decrease in the latter months.

In October, a St. John's man was slapped with a $10,000 fine for possession of contraband. He was stopped on the highway coming up from the Burin Peninsula with 458 tubs of tobacco that originated in St. Pierre. This was, up to that date, one of the largest fines ever for possession of illegally imported goods.

In the same month, three men from St. Lawrence and one from Little St. Lawrence were arrested following a chase of a twenty-foot fibreglass boat by an RCMP patrol vessel, about seven kilometres south of St. Lawrence.

Contraband seized in that particular incident included 150 tubs of tobacco, eighty-eight cartons of cigarettes, and six bottles of liquor. The boat was also seized by the police.

It was stated that, with the right connections, contraband tobacco and alcohol could be obtained in virtually any town in the province.

The RCMP were stating that a number of well-organized groups handled smuggling on the Newfoundland end. The era had changed when a fisherman slipped across to St. Pierre to get a few cases of liquor for his neighbours and himself. That era is long over.

Now it was estimated that roughly fifty boats were involved in smuggling operations on a regular basis.

Moratoriums and quota cuts had left idle hundreds of fishermen on the Burin Peninsula. However, the fishery crisis hadn't led to a smuggling upswing. Fishermen in general weren't involved in commercial smuggling. Ninety per cent of smugglers had never jigged a fish in their life. They were smugglers first and foremost.

December 1993 was true to tradition. In the early part of the month, an RCMP patrol was attempting to stop a pickup truck between Fortune and Point May, when the driver jumped from the moving vehicle and fled into the woods. The truck went over a fifty-foot embankment and rolled over on its side, spilling 113 cases of liquor and fifteen cases of tobacco. The seizure was estimated to be valued at $52,000. A twenty-four-year-old St. Lawrence man was later apprehended.

In another incident, RCMP in English Harbour West found a stash near the graveyard of that community. Eighty-four cases of liquor and forty-two cases of tobacco were found, but no arrests were made in that incident.

A few days before Christmas, RCMP from St. Lawrence, along with members of the Burin Customs and Excise Section assisted by a police dog, were conducting searches for contraband goods in several private homes and a wooded area near the community of Lord's Cove.

The officers had seized several cases of tobacco and liquor when a large crowd gathered around the police vehicles. Tires were slashed on two vehicles and a rear window was smashed. RCMP also alleged that a man waved a knife at the police dog and threatened his trainer. This was the second such incident in a year when encounters with the police had come close to erupting into a riot.

The stepped-up enforcement was resulting in numerous

seizures, which wasn't to everyone's liking. In fact, at year's end, statistics showed that police had confiscated a total of $1,500,000 according to fair market value.

In 1993, only 6,000 tubs of tobacco were confiscated. The number had increased from 325 in 1992. In 1992, there had been 5,450 litres of alcohol seized, while in 1993 there had been 16,000 litres. Vehicles confiscated had risen from fifteen in 1992 to fifty-one in 1993. Things were really starting to clamp down. How much longer would this trade be able to survive?

Rumrunning boat seized by RCMP on Burin Peninsula.
(Author collection)

SMUGGLING IN 1994

In early January 1994, the RCMP patrol vessel *Fort McCloud* and an RCMP speedboat were on patrol just off the boot of the Burin Peninsula.

They intercepted a small boat with two masked men aboard, which they alleged to have been engaged in smuggling liquor and tobacco products from St. Pierre.

When the rumrunners on board the small craft spotted the police, they made a 180-degree turn and headed back toward St. Pierre, with both RCMP vessels in hot pursuit. The rumrunners ignored all police warnings to halt.

The arrival of the alleged would-be smugglers pursued by one of the RCMP boats back into St. Pierre Harbour created quite a stir.

St. Pierre residents actually assisted the Newfoundlanders, who abandoned their vessel and alleged cargo of contraband as they leaped from the boat to the wharf. The St. Pierre residents secured the craft and brought its cargo ashore. Meanwhile, the RCMP were trying to take possession of the rumrunning craft, but were stopped by some St. Pierre residents who took oars from a nearby boat and started to wave them in the direction of the police to stop them from doing so.

The RCMP finally decided to exit without their prize.

The RCMP had been in clear violation of international law by having crossed the territorial boundaries of the French-owned islands to try to arrest the rumrunners in the harbour. These types of incidents were not frequent. There had been another intrusion in the late 1960s of an RCMP patrol vessel in search of a rumrunner. They had no authorization to come into French territorial waters, and in spite of instructions from French customs to come alongside, the captain had ignored their instructions and had left the harbour after ascertaining that there was no one he was interested in. The captain of the vessel had allegedly been dismissed as a result of the incident.

The RCMP stated that they considered the latest incident unfortunate and expressed their regrets to St. Pierre government officials.

The case was far from over, and the police were not about to be defeated by this embarrassing incident, which could have led to a protest and exchange of diplomatic notes between France and Canada.

As a result, two weeks later, they formally charged two brothers from St. Lawrence with smuggling and obstructing a police officer in the course of his duty. This was acceptable; the Mounties may go to any extreme to get their man, but they had better not go to St. Pierre and Miquelon.

When the case was finally disposed of two years later, in May 1996, the Mounties found out the hard way that the "hot pursuit" defence was useless when the chase took them across an international boundary.

A judge in Grand Bank threw out the evidence after determining the Mounties broke the international law of the sea.

It was revealed in court that the RCMP boat was in such close proximity to the rumrunning vessel that the individuals on board were fending them off with equipment.

It was also stated that the Mounties pressed on, following the rumrunners across the international boundary and all the way to St. Pierre Harbour, where one officer had jumped on the rumrunning vessel, had torn open a green garbage bag, and found contraband tobacco.

Two individuals had been charged with smuggling alcohol and tobacco products into Newfoundland, although the Mounties hadn't seized any contraband, nor had they arrested the alleged rumrunners in St. Pierre.

Police argued in court that under Section 477 of the Criminal Code of Canada, enforcement officers may continue a chase outside Canadian waters if they are in hot pursuit of suspected criminals.

True, the judge noted, but only when the chase takes them into international waters.

St. Pierre, of course, is in French territorial waters.

The judge, in throwing the case out of court, noted, "I am of the opinion that it would be inappropriate to admit this evidence, as to do so would be to endorse behaviour contrary to international law." The judge further added, "Agents of government must recognize there is a limit to their authority."

This put an end to yet another variation on the history of police versus the rumrunners.

In February 1994, two men and a woman from Lawn and a man from Chapel Arm were arrested following a long investigation by the RCMP. Police said that during the course of their six-month investigation, they seized 557 200-gram tubs of tobacco, 464 1.75-litre bottles of liquor, and 109 cartons of cigarettes, with a total street value of $54,000.

In February 1994, it had been announced that ten additional Mounties would join the effort to stop the smuggling taking place between Newfoundland and St. Pierre.

The new officers were a gift to the province from Ottawa, and tied to a federal anti-smuggling campaign that included tax cuts and a doubling of anti-smuggling officers.

In Newfoundland that translated into ten officers plus two support staff, who were to join the team of eight Mounties already involved in anti-smuggling activities.

These new measures still didn't stop attempts to bring the goods to market. On February 12, a successful search on the Burin highway turned up 349 tins of tobacco in the trunk of a car. The street value was estimated at $14,000. When the Lord's Cove resident went to court, he was fined $1,000 on the charge of possession of contraband, and levied a tax evasion penalty of $23,906. In addition, one of the man's vehicles was forfeited to the Crown. In default of paying the fine, he would have to serve seven months in jail.

April 1994 was a good month for the RCMP, but a sad one for the smugglers. Within a few days, police were able to seize about $100,000 worth of contraband. They stopped a truck in Lewin's Cove containing fifty-two cases of tobacco with a street value of $52,000. The driver fled on foot and escaped to the woods. The same day, the police seized a nine-year-old Chevrolet Caprice vehicle in the community of Lawn, loaded with 180 1.75-litre bottles of liquor valued at $8,100. Meanwhile, 420 tins of tobacco with a value of $15,000 were seized in the south coast community of Belleoram.

In May 1994, the RCMP seized an abandoned van full of liquor and tobacco. The van, which had been rented in Marystown, contained 136 cases of contraband liquor and ten cases of tobacco, for a total value of $52,000.

There were no arrests in connection with this seizure, which took place at 2:40 a.m. near Red Harbour. The occupants of the van were able to flee before the RCMP arrived on the scene. It is believed that the smugglers were tipped off that the Mounties were patrolling in the area.

In September 1994, in Creston South, police seized $66,000 worth of contraband, a twenty-three-foot fibreglass boat valued at $25,000, and a pickup truck. Contraband seized included twenty-seven cases of tobacco, two cases of cigarettes, and eighty-eight cases of liquor.

* * *

Later that month, seven people were arrested after more than thirty RCMP officers swooped down on the community of Terrenceville in a crackdown which capped a lengthy investigation into tobacco and alcohol smuggling from St. Pierre.

The police stated that it was the largest seizure and restraint of assets ever undertaken in Newfoundland.

Police seized a large quantity of contraband, placed restraining orders on three homes, seized four boats, six vehicles and pickup trucks, ATVs, snowmobiles, and dirt bikes.

For the first time ever in Newfoundland, RCMP applied the provisions of the new "proceeds of crime" legislation to help combat the smuggling of liquor and tobacco products.

The recently approved legislation was enacted to provide for the seizure, restitution, and forfeiture of assets acquired through unlawful means.

The RCMP, armed with a boom truck, a flatbed transport truck, and trailers, moved in the early hours of the morning. They loaded the seized goods onto the large vehicle and hauled it away.

Police stated that under the proceeds of the crime act, if police suspect that someone has acquired proceeds, be it a house, car, money in a bank account, or any other tangible asset through criminal offences, it could now be rightfully seized by the police. The property would become a ward of the state until the matter was heard in court.

The Terrenceville raid was the culmination of an eight-month investigation code-named Operation Bacon. The total value of the contraband and assets seized was over $300,000.

Operation Bacon was probably the biggest blow to the rumrunning circuits on the Burin Peninsula. Rumrunners were faced with the prospect of losing everything they owned. Those who wished to continue in the trade had to re-evaluate their strategies. Money that was made couldn't be put into a bank account; it had to be buried in the garden, or it could be seized. Rumrunners who had assets would have to use young men without assets as fronts so as not to lose their properties.

Operation Bacon had not killed the rumrunning trade but had put a serious dent into it.

Instead of dozens of speedboats loading up contraband in St. Pierre, the trade had suddenly fallen to a handful of boats.

The police, on the other hand, were happy since they felt the Terrenceville bust would do more to curb smuggling than anything previously attempted, and they were right.

With confiscation of goods purchased with what police referred to as smugglers' ill-gotten gains, the balance had been shifted drastically. Now police felt that they had the upper hand and that smuggling had now become a high-risk venture.

Seized tobacco and alcohol on the Burin Peninsula.
(Author collection)

Top and bottom: RCMP roadblock on the Burin highway in attempt to seize contraband alcohol and tobacco. (Author collection)

SMUGGLING IN 1995

The bad news for rumrunners was not over yet. The RCMP announced that a high-speed catamaran would be introduced in the summer of 1995. The commissioning of this new vessel was to serve as an additional strong deterrent for would-be smugglers.

The new vessel was to be equipped with state-of-the-art automatic radar plotting that could pinpoint a vessel and give course and speed. The biggest advantage would be the speed of the new police vessel, which would be capable of a top speed of thirty-eight knots with good manoeuvrability.

All of this dampened the spirits of smugglers somewhat, but didn't stop the traditional rumrunning activities. In March 1995, a resident of Allan's Island was charged with possession of 120 1.75-litre bottles of liquor valued at $6,000. The RCMP also seized his ten-year-old Dodge Aries which was used to transport the goods to market.

During the same week, police recovered contraband on the shoreline near Point May. Goods included 162 1.75-litre bottles of assorted liquor, twenty-six five-litre jugs of pure alcohol, thirty-two tins of tobacco, and twelve cartons of cigarettes.

In April 1995, the Canadian Coast Guard gave new meaning to the term "search and rescue."

Two men from Bellevue were charged after being rescued from their vessel about eight kilometres south of St. Lawrence.

Their boat had developed engine trouble during the night and activated its emergency signal, which was picked up by the St. Lawrence Coastal Radio station. They in turn notified Search and Rescue, which dispatched a helicopter from the SAR Squadron in Gander.

The helicopter spotted the disabled craft and relayed its location to the Coast Guard vessel in Burin, which towed the vessel to port.

Members of the RCMP and Customs and Excise Section boarded the craft and found some contraband liquor stored in the stern section.

Police impounded the vessel, liquor, and equipment.

The same month, on a Fortune nightclub parking lot, police also seized a vehicle containing a quantity of contraband liquor and tobacco products. A Grand Bank woman was subsequently charged and went to trial, where she was convicted and fined $1,000 each under the liquor control act and the provincial tobacco tax act. She was fined an additional $28,965 for tax assessments on the smuggled goods.

In May, police swooped down by helicopter on the isolated community of Rencontre East, where they found in a storage shed on a wharf 330 1.75-litre bottles of liquor, thirty-nine tubs of tobacco, fifty cartons of cigarettes, and two five-litre jugs of pure alcohol, with a total value of $33,000.

OPERATION BUFFER

In mid-May 1995, before dawn, police raided homes across eastern and southern Newfoundland, laying smuggling charges.

The raids began on the Burin Peninsula, with a convoy of fifteen to twenty police cars converging on St. Lawrence shortly before 5:00 a.m. The task force made arrests and seized assets under the proceeds-of-crime legislation.

Known as Operation Buffer, the sweep involved the seizure of thousands of dollars in goods allegedly obtained through smuggling liquor and tobacco from St. Pierre.

In one instance, the police broke into the wrong house during their raid. The Mounties entered a home, banged on the walls, and made a lot of noise. When they realized they had the wrong house, they left without an apology, telling the owner that "these things happen." Other raids took place in Lawn and Lord's Cove.

Several other homes were raided on the Avalon Peninsula and other parts of eastern and southern Newfoundland.

In all, twenty-four people were arrested and a total of $750,000 worth of property seized or restrained in the largest anti-smuggling investigation ever undertaken in Newfoundland.

The police investigation had begun a year and a half previously and involved the use of wiretap procedures.

The total number of charges against those arrested in Operation Buffer was estimated to have exceeded 100. The charges included conspiracy to sell contraband, evasion of duties under the Customs

Act, and other related charges. Assets restrained in the operation included three homes, four vehicles, two twenty-five-foot boats, one snowmobile, two rental properties, and two cottages.

Police admitted after this latest operation that they might not be able to totally stop the smuggling trade from St. Pierre to Newfoundland, but they could increase the risk for those involved.

In the good old days prior to the proceeds-of-crime legislation, the risk factors, fines, and periods of incarceration were deemed acceptable as the price paid for doing business, but now it was no longer the case.

Despite Operation Buffer, some limited amount of liquor and tobacco continued to filter through the cracks of the system.

* * *

In the first half of September, the *Simmonds*, the RCMP's newest commissioned patrol vessel, arrived in Burin and was described as ready to start pursuit of smugglers.

It was announced that people on Newfoundland's south coast who persisted in smuggling contraband liquor and tobacco from St. Pierre and Miquelon would have a newer, faster obstacle to contend with.

In November 1995, the RCMP Customs and Excise Section searched a shed in Terrenceville and seized a significant quantity of contraband liquor and tobacco products.

Seized were 360 1.75-litre bottles of liquor, as well as 240 tubs of tobacco, and fifty cartons of cigarettes.

The same month, nine Burin Peninsula residents were fined more than $16,000 when they pleaded guilty to contraband charges in provincial court in Grand Bank.

OPERATION DIAMOND

In December 1995, the RCMP, the Royal Newfoundland Constabulary, and the Newfoundland and Labrador Liquor Corporation's enforcement section raided eleven bars across the province that were suspected of retailing contraband liquor.

This resulted from a seven-month investigation, and concluded with the seizure of liquor and accounting journals from bars on the Burin Peninsula, St. John's, Torbay, Stephenville, Gander, and Bryant's Cove near Harbour Grace.

The investigation, dubbed Operation Diamond, devoted a new approach by the liquor corporation to become more actively involved in addressing the serious problems created by the illegal importation of contraband liquor from St. Pierre and Miquelon.

The investigation included desk audits, field audits, and the introduction of new scientific equipment that could readily identify the properties of alcoholic beverages.

This meant that they now had the means to identify an alcoholic beverage that had been transferred from an illegal bottle to a legal bottle.

If convicted, the bars faced lengthy licence suspensions or charges under the liquor control act.

On Christmas Eve, 1995, a Marystown man was driving a 1985 Ford Ranger on Route 210 near Marystown, when he was pulled over by members of the Customs and Excise Section of the RCMP.

The car was loaded with 210 tubs of tobacco, as well as 100 cartons of cigarettes, with a street value of $15,000.

The RCMP sent him home for Christmas without his car, with orders to appear in court in February.

* * *

In January 1996, a resident of Creston South was convicted in Supreme Court in Grand Bank of unlawful possession of contraband liquor and tobacco.

He was fined $5,500 as a result of the seizure of contraband valued at $66,000, and he lost his boat and truck, which were forfeited for an additional value of $28,000.

A co-accused from Winterland was fined a total of $22,505 after pleading guilty. These were pretty hefty fines. This was the culmination of a September 1994 case. These heavy penalties had somehow started to slow down the process, and there was a substantially lesser amount of cases before the courts.

In February 1996, four additional Burin Peninsula men were convicted of liquor and tobacco offences. One was fined $34,700 or seven months in jail, the second $10,000 or six months in jail, the third $5,000 or two months in jail, and the fourth $8,600 or four months in jail.

In April 1996, the four residents of Terrenceville charged in connection with Operation Bacon in October went to trial, and all four pleaded guilty.

They had been charged with conspiracy to import contraband products into Canada from St. Pierre and Miquelon, and were also charged with possession of contraband goods under the so-called "proceeds of crime" legislation. This was the first ever application of the proceeds-of-crime laws toward an offence of smuggling in Newfoundland. The RCMP had seized assets valued at approximately $300,000.

The first was fined $13,000, or in default, one year in jail, the second $10,000 or one year in jail, the third $5,940 or six months in jail, and the fourth $3,300 or five months in jail. All of their assets were ordered forfeited and ordered put up for sale. This was the biggest forfeiture in a case concerning illicit importation of alcohol and tobacco from St. Pierre.

The Terrenceville case had been the determining factor in bringing these smuggling operations down to a trickle.

On May 3, 1996, RCMP officers were bringing a six-month smuggling investigation to a conclusion in Grey River on the southwest coast when they ran into an unexpected impediment, a barrier of men.

Officers moved in on the community near midnight and arrested a resident, seizing forty-five cases of liquor valued at $21,500, and a twenty-two-foot boat valued at $13,000. The liquor was allegedly smuggled in from Miquelon, which is closer to Grey River than St. Pierre.

There were more arrests and seizures to come, but as they were carrying out their plan in the early morning hours, they were confronted by a group of about fifteen men.

The officers called for backup to come to this isolated community. When the RCMP patrol vessel *Simmonds* arrived, five other suspects were arrested within a few hours.

In June of 1996, an RCMP fast-rescue craft intercepted a twenty-two-foot fibreglass boat off English Harbour West around 11:00 p.m. The boat, loaded with contraband, was seized a short time later following a brief chase.

Two men, one from Terrenceville and one from English Harbour East, were taken into custody and escorted back to Grand Bank.

The Mounties confiscated 570 200-gram tubs of tobacco, 465 1.75-litre bottles of assorted liquors, and twenty-eight cartons of cigarettes, valued at $50,000.

When the accused faced the court the following month, they were respectively fined $12,000 or six months in jail, and $10,000 or five months in jail.

In June 1996, seventeen people were arrested in three areas of the province on smuggling charges.

About fifty RCMP officers moved in by land, sea, and air on homes in Fortune Bay, Grand Falls, Windsor, and Paradise.

Seized during the raid was a boat valued at $7,500, and in excess of $20,000 in property allegedly used to commit a crime or obtained from proceeds of crime. A quantity of liquor and tobacco was seized during the arrest. A second vessel was also seized that police say was previously involved in the investigation.

The operation involved the interception of communications of several individuals, and culminated in arrests and seizures.

In October 1996, the RCMP Customs and Excise Section adopted a new approach to help combat what they deemed as the unacceptable level of smuggling liquor and tobacco products in Newfoundland.

The police released a new video dramatizing the effects of this smuggling activity on society in an all-out effort to make people more aware of the problems and effects of this unlawful activity on society.

An RCMP spokesman admitted that smuggling was a historic problem along the south coast of the province which had escalated dramatically since 1988.

This was a blatant admission that it had been a big mistake to take the patrol vessel *Centennial* out of service in April of 1988, which had left the door wide open to the rumrunning trade.

To make up for lost time, the police had responded with a series of initiatives, and among them was a decision to dedicate significant RCMP resources to anti-smuggling enforcement in the province. In order to underline the significance of the problem, the police wanted to dispel the perception that smuggling was an innocuous game, with no victims.

In late November 1996, combined forces arrested six Burin Peninsula men on charges of conspiracy to smuggle contraband. The arrests were a result of a six-month undercover investigation coded-named Operation Bruno. The RCMP seized a total of $31,000 of contraband goods, along with three vehicles, an ATV, and a utility trailer that police alleged was used to transport the goods. The contraband included 675 200-gram tins of tobacco, and sixty-five 1.75-litre bottles of liquor.

All these seizures made it more and more difficult to complete successful rumrunning operations. The once-flourishing trade had almost been brought to a standstill. In 1997, the sophisticated, ever-increasing police presence must have scared the would-be rumrunners, since only a handful of seizures could be reported.

In September 1997, the RCMP, assisted by the police service dog, Buddy, uncovered 700 1.75-litre bottles of liquor, and 130 200-gram tubs of tobacco, following a search near the Anglican Church graveyard in Lamaline.

The stash was hidden in tall grass along the cemetery fence. The total value of the seizure was $44,000; no owners of the goods were identified.

In a similar story, on Christmas Eve, 1997, police seized fifty-two cases of assorted liquor and seventeen cases of tobacco on a beach in Pie Duck Cove near Point May. The total value of goods seized was $40,000. An investigation was carried out in an attempt to determine who owned the unclaimed contraband.

Close by, in the neighbouring community of Lawn, a retired schoolteacher fifty-five years of age was allegedly murdered and her house set on fire. The crime was discovered, and in their investigation to find the responsible individual, police found in one of the residences $75,000 of contraband.

In December 1998, it was felt that the forthcoming Christmas could be the driest on record for residents of the Burin Peninsula, as far as smuggled liquor was concerned.

It was felt that there was hardly a drop of contraband liquor available. The main reason was the crackdown by the RCMP Burin Peninsula Customs and Excise Section.

The addition of the high-speed patrol vessel *Simmonds*, combined with increased intelligence, stepped-up onshore surveillance, and Crime Stoppers promotions has had a major impact. Stiffer fines and penalties arising from the introduction of proceeds-of-crime legislation, in liquor and tobacco smuggling cases, also had a major impact on bringing a definite end to these operations.

AFTERWORD

As this final chapter of this book was written, the illegal liquor trade for all intents and purposes was gone.

It had been a common occurrence to see fifteen to twenty boats a night loading up. Now, one or two boats may show up once in a while, taking small quantities of liquor for their own consumption.

These new enforcement methods have put an end to smuggling operations that were ongoing since the 1800s and that peaked with the Prohibition era.

This has resulted in increased sales of legal liquor and tobacco products on the south coast of Newfoundland.

ACKNOWLEDGEMENTS

A special thank you to Mr. Henri Moraze, who gave me access to his personal archives of the Prohibition era, to the Briand-Ozon family, Mrs. Yvonne Andrieux, Lucien Girardin Dagort, Mr Andre Bechet, Eugene Levavasseur, Mrs. Marie Enguehard, Clem Cusick, Gustave Roblot, Jean Apesteguy, Emile Derrible of St. Pierre, and to Captain R. C. Butt, Mr. James Miller, Mr. Bob Power, Dr. G. Robinson, Graham McBride of the Maritime Museum of Halifax, to Ms. Jamie Seran of the Yarmouth County Museum, and to many others too numerous to mention, without whose help and assistance this book would not have been possible.

BIBLIOGRAPHY

Gray, James H. *Booze: The Impact of Whisky on the Prairie West.* Scarborough, ON: New American Library of Canada, 1972.

Louis-Legasse, Ferdinand. *Evolution économique des Iles Saint-Pierre et Miquelon.* Sirey, Paris: Librairie du Receuil, 1935.

Moraze, Henri. Personal archives, letters, and documents (unpublished).

Newman, Peter C. *Bronfman Dynasty: The Rothschilds of the New World.* Toronto: McClelland & Stewart, 1978.

Pinaquy, Joseph. Personal journal on Saint-Pierre et Miquelon, 1887–1922 (unpublished).

Prowse, D. W. *A History of Newfoundland.* London: Macmillan, 1895.

Robinson, Geoff, and Dorothy Robinson. *Duty Free.* Summerside, PE: Alpha Graphics, 1992.

———. *It Came by the Boat Load.* Summerside, PE: Alpha Graphics, 1984.

St. John's Daily News (various articles)

St. John's Telegram (various articles).

Van de Water, Frederic. *The Real McCoy*. Garden City, NY: Doubleday, Doran & Company, 1931.

Willoughby, Malcolm F. *Rum War at Sea*. Washington, DC: United States Government Printing Office, 1964.

INDEX

ABOUT THE AUTHOR

Jean Pierre Andrieux is a St. John's–based businessman and author of several books published since 1970.

He was born in Montreal of St. Pierre–Miquelon parents, raised in Prince Edward Island, and graduated from the Sir George William's University School of Retailing (now Concordia) in 1968. He has been closely linked to the tourism industry both in St. Pierre and Newfoundland since that time.

Andrieux has a photo collection that exceeds 30,000 prints and is regularly a guest lecturer on cruise vessels. He is the Honorary Vice Consul of Spain for Newfoundland and Labrador. He is married to Elizabeth King, and they reside in St. John's.